MIND WAR

HOW MEN & WOMEN THINK DIFFERENTLY

MAHESHKUMAR BHOSLE

BlueRose ONE .com
Stories Matter
NewDelhi • London

BLUEROSE PUBLISHERS
India | U.K.

BlueRoseONE.com
Stories Matter
NewDelhi • London

For permissions requests or inquiries regarding this publication, please contact:

BLUEROSE PUBLISHERS
www.BlueRoseONE.com
info@bluerosepublishers.com
+91 8882 898 898
+4407342408967

ISBN: 978-93-7542-541-0

Cover design: Maheshkumar Bhosle

Typesetting: Tanya Raj Upadhyay

First Edition: February 2026

SUMMARY

Title: Mind War of Women and Men

"Mind War of Women and Men" is a bold and thought-provoking book that explores the deep mental and emotional differences between men and women. Through engaging dialogue, real-life situations, and relatable examples, this book examines how both genders think, react, and communicate differently in various aspects of life—relationships, parenting, shopping, decision-making, and emotions.

The book does not aim to blame either side but rather seeks to bridge the gap in understanding. It highlights the silent battles fought inside the minds of both women and men, often misunderstood by each other. Each chapter reveals how small differences in thinking can lead to big misunderstandings—and how awareness can lead to better harmony.

Whether you're a husband or wife, boyfriend or girlfriend, or just curious about human psychology, this book offers eye-opening insights with a mix of humour, reality, and heart. Why do men and women often fail to understand each other – even when they deeply care? Why does a simple conversation turn into an argument?

Why do men stay silent while women want to talk it out?

Mind War of Women and Men is not just a book—it's a mirror that reflects how both genders think differently and why that difference often leads to confusion, emotional clashes, or distance. Based on everyday examples, the book dives into the mental and emotional workings of women and men, uncovering patterns shaped by biology, culture, emotions, and upbringing.

Each chapter focuses on a theme like:

How women and men argue differently

Why shopping becomes a battlefield

Parenting approaches from each side

Emotional expression vs emotional control

Decision-making styles

How love is felt and shown differently

The book uses conversations, real-life inspired stories, and simple language to present the unseen 'mind wars' both genders fight daily—often without realizing it. It shows how misunderstandings grow not because of hate or ego, but because the thinking process itself is different. encourages readers to understand, respect, and work with these differences. The goal is not war—but wisdom.

Anyone curious about gender psychology.

Whether you're looking for clarity, a bit of humour, or real-life advice, Mind War of Women and Men opens the door to a deeper understanding of the opposite mind.

Dedicated To

"This book is dedicated to all men and women – two unique minds, two different worlds, yet bound by the same human spirit. It is for those who seek to understand, not to judge; to listen, not to argue; to bridge the gap between thoughts and emotions. May these pages inspire respect, empathy, and harmony between the genders, reminding us that our differences are not walls but doors to deeper connection."

A Special thanks to my school friend, Dr. Raviraj Gitte(Laparoscopic Surgeon), for his honest suggestions, intellectual inputs, and encouragement throughout the Journey of this Book.

"Two Minds, One World"

She thinks in colours, he thinks in lines,
She hears the rhythm; he sees the signs.
He walks with logic, cool and clear,
She flies with feeling, far and near.

He holds the map, reads every mark,
she lights the path with inner spark.
He builds the frame, firm and tight,
She fills it all with warmth and light.

He guards his silence, deep and wide,
She tells her truth, with none to hide.
He may not cry, but he feels deep,
She may seem soft, but her strength will keep.

She dreams aloud, he dreams in code,
Yet love is built on this shared road.
Different minds, but hearts align—
In every clash, a grand design.

Why Men and Women Think Differently

Biological Factors

- Brain Structure & Connectivity: On average, men's brains tend to have more connections within each hemisphere, which can support focused, analytical tasks. Women's brains often show stronger cross-hemisphere connections, which may facilitate multitasking and communication. However, these differences are averages with significant overlap, and individual variation is greater than gender differences.
- Hormones: Testosterone, estrogen, and oxytocin influence brain development and behaviour. For example, testosterone is linked to risk-taking and competitiveness, while oxytocin promotes bonding and empathy. Hormonal levels fluctuate across life stages and situations, affecting cognition and mood in complex ways.

Psychological and Emotional Processing

- Emotional Expression: Women generally score higher on emotional recognition and empathy tests, which can influence communication and decision-making styles. Men may tend toward problem-solving approaches, often shaped by social expectations about masculinity.

- Decision-Making and Risk: Men often take more risks on average, partially influenced by biology and partly by cultural reinforcement. Women tend to use more intuition and social cues in decisions, although again, there is broad individual variation.

Social and Cultural Influences

- From early childhood, boys and girls are often socialized differently–through toys, schooling, media, and family roles–which shapes thinking patterns and skills. For example, girls may be encouraged to develop verbal and relational skills, while boys may be pushed toward spatial and mechanical tasks.
- Gender Roles and Expectations: Over time, these societal pressures can reinforce differences in how men and women approach problem-solving, communication, and emotional expression.

Think Differently (Discussion)

- The brain is highly adaptable. Experiences, training, and environments shape neural connections, often reinforcing or minimizing initial biological differences. For example, women in leadership roles may develop stronger strategic thinking skills; men in caregiving roles may enhance empathy-related brain functions.
- Men and women think differently not just because of biology, but because of a dynamic interplay between hormones, brain structure, psychology, and cultural environment. The differences are tendencies, not rules–individual experiences and choices shape our minds far more than gender alone.

Table of Contents

Part I: The Biological Battlefield

Chapter 1: Wired Differently? The Brain and Gender

- Brain size myths
- Hemispheric specialization
- Neural connectivity studies
- Additional Insights on Brain Plasticity and Gender

Chapter 2: The Hormonal Influence

- Testosterone, estrogen, oxytocin
- Hormones and behaviour
- Impact of menstrual cycle, puberty, and menopause

Chapter 3: Evolutionary Psychology and Survival Thinking

- Gender roles in evolution
- Risk-taking and aggression

Empathy and caregiving

Chapter 1:
Wired Differently? The Brain and Gender

Chapter Goal:

To explore key concepts in brain science, beginning with myths about brain size and intelligence.

Understand how hemispheric specialization influences behaviour without oversimplifying brain functions.

Examine the importance of neural connectivity over individual brain regions.

Highlight the brain's remarkable plasticity and its ability to change with experience.

This topic aims to deepen understanding of how structure and function shape the human mind.

- Brain size myths
- Hemispheric specialization
- Neural connectivity studies
- Plasticity: brains change with experience

Section 1: Brain Size Myths

- The myth: "Men have bigger brains, so they're smarter."

- Reality: Men do have larger brains on average due to larger body size, but intelligence does not correlate with brain size.
- What actually matters: Neuron density, white vs. Gray matter ratios, efficiency of networks.
- Fun fact: Einstein's brain was smaller than average but had a higher density of glial cells in certain areas.
- It's a myth that larger brains mean greater intelligence or that male brains are inherently superior due to size.
- While male brains are, on average, slightly larger than female brains, this difference does not correlate with intelligence or cognitive ability.
- The size difference is proportionate to overall body size, not mental capacity.
- Historically, people believed that brain size equals intelligence, and since male brains are often slightly larger (due to larger average body size), this was misinterpreted to mean men were smarter.
- Modern neuroscience has shown that intelligence isn't linked to brain size. What matters more are factors like:
    - The efficiency of brain networks.
    - How well different brain regions communicate?
    - The density and organization of neurons (not just volume).

- Also, female brains tend to have more connections per cubic centimetre of brain tissue, showing different but equally complex organization.
- Reality: Male brains are, on average, about 10% larger than female brains. This difference is mainly due to body size, not intelligence.
- Key point: Intelligence depends more on how the brain is organized and used, not its size.
- Research: Studies show no meaningful link between brain volume and cognitive ability. Both males and females can perform equally well on IQ and other thinking-related tasks.
- Male brains are slightly larger on average, but size doesn't determine intelligence.
- Brain efficiency and connectivity matter more than volume
- Intelligence depends on:
- Neural efficiency: how fast and effectively the brain processes info.
- Synaptic connections: how neurons link and communicate.
- Brain region density: especially in the prefrontal cortex, tied to decision-making and reasoning.
- Women's brains are often more tightly packed with neurons in certain areas, which helps balance out the size difference.

- In the 19th century, scientists used skull measurements to argue women were inferior—a practice now known as craniometry.
- This was deeply biased "science" that supported sexist views, not real biology.
- These outdated ideas were later disproven, but their influence lingered in education and science for decades.
- Surprising Fact: Some Small-Brained People Are Geniuses
- Some individuals with hydrocephalus (a condition that reduces brain volume) have very high IQs, showing brain adaptability is more important than size.
- One famous case: a man had only 10% of a normal brain volume, yet earned a math degree and lived a normal life!
- The Brain Is a Super-Efficient Machine
- The human brain, regardless of gender, weighs around 3 pounds but uses 20% of your body's energy.
- It can form up to 1,000 trillion connections (synapses)—and it constantly rewires itself as you learn.

Section 2: Hemispheric Specialization

- Old claim: "Men use one side of the brain; women use both."

- Scientific nuance:
- Studies show some lateralization differences (language functions, for example), but it's not as binary as pop science suggests.
- Brain function is distributed and redundant.
- Common misconception: Left brain = logical; Right brain = emotional. (Over-simplified.)
- Popular but oversimplified and not supported by strong scientific evidence.
- Hemispheric specialization, also known as lateralization of brain function, refers to the idea that the two hemispheres of the brain are specialized for different types of tasks.

1. Left Hemisphere Functions
    - Language processing: Includes Broca's area (speech production) and Wernicke's area (language comprehension)
    - Analytical thinking: Logical reasoning, mathematics
    - Sequential processing: Deals with information in a step-by-step manner
    - Right-hand control: Controls the right side of the body
2. Right Hemisphere Functions
    - Spatial abilities: Visual and spatial processing, such as recognizing faces and understanding maps
    - Creativity and intuition: Artistic and musical abilities

- Emotional processing: Especially interpreting tone of voice and facial expressions
- Left-hand control: Controls the left side of the body

3. Popular myth, not fully supported by research.

- Some studies show small sex differences in brain lateralization, but they are not significant or consistent.
- Scientific view: Some brain functions (like language) show lateralization, but both hemispheres usually work together.
- Misconception: "Left = logic, Right = emotion" – Too simplistic.
- The brain is complex, distributed, and often redundant in its functions.
- A. Scientific Nuance
- Some lateralization exists, especially in areas like language processing.
- Differences between sexes are minor and not absolute.
- Brain function is distributed across both hemispheres.
- The brain is redundant and adaptive, with many functions involving inter-hemispheric cooperation.
- B. Common Misconception
- Left brain = logical

- Right brain = emotional
- This dichotomy is over-simplified.
- While certain functions are more dominant in one hemisphere, both sides are involved in most complex tasks.
- C. Scientific Understanding
- Lateralization: Some brain functions are more dominant in one hemisphere.
- Left hemisphere: Often associated with language, logic, and analytical thinking.
- Right hemisphere: Often associated with spatial awareness, creativity, and emotional processing.
- However, both hemispheres work together for most tasks.
- Example: Understanding speech involves left-hemisphere language areas and right-hemisphere tone/emotion processing.
- Brain function is distributed and redundant:
    - Many processes involve multiple areas across both hemispheres.
    - If one side is damaged, the other can sometimes compensate (neuroplasticity).

D. Common Misconception

- Left brain = logical, Right brain = emotional
- This idea is over-simplified.

- While there are patterns of specialization, no one is truly "left-brained" or "right-brained."
- Both hemispheres are active during most cognitive and emotional activities.

E. Split-Brain Research

- Studies on patients who had their corpus callosum (the structure connecting the two hemispheres) severed to treat severe epilepsy
- Key findings:
    - When the hemispheres cannot communicate, each side operates independently
    - Example: A split-brain patient may be able to name an object seen with the right visual field (left hemisphere) but not one seen in the left visual field (right hemisphere)

F. Integration of Hemispheres

- Despite specialization, both hemispheres typically work together
- The corpus callosum allows for communication between hemispheres
- Tasks often require input from both sides (e.g., conversation involves both language and emotional tone)

Section 3: Neural Connectivity Studies

- Viral headlines: "Male brains are wired front-to-back, female brains side-to-side."

- Closer look:
    - Yes, some connectivity patterns differ on average–but with massive overlap between sexes.
    - What's often ignored: individual variation outweighs gender averages.
    - Task-specific performance is a better predictor of connectivity than gender.
- Partial truth: Some studies, including large-scale brain scans, show average differences in neural connectivity between sexes.
- Key context missing: These differences show significant overlap–many individuals don't conform to the "typical" pattern for their sex.
- Bigger picture: Individual variation in brain wiring is far more pronounced than sex-based averages.
- Better predictor: Brain connectivity correlates more with task-specific demands (like motor skills or memory tasks) than with gender.

Section 4: Additional Insights on Brain Plasticity and Gender

A. Neuroplasticity Across the Lifespan

- Plasticity isn't limited to childhood–the adult brain remains flexible.
- Activities like learning a language, playing an instrument, or starting a new job continue to reshape neural pathways well into old age.

- This means life stages (e.g., parenting, career changes) can significantly affect brain structure and function—regardless of gender.

B. Experience Over Biology

- Studies show that practice and environment often override sex-based differences.
    - E.g., men and women trained in the same task (like spatial navigation or empathy-focused caregiving) tend to develop similar brain changes.
- The brain adapts to what it's used for, not necessarily to the person's sex.

C. Social Role Influence

- Cultural roles (like "provider" or "nurturer") come with different daily challenges that train different brain functions.
- As societal norms shift and roles diversify, the range of experiences influencing brain development also broadens across genders.

D. Plasticity Undermines Determinism

- If brain wiring changes with use, then fixed ideas about "male brains" or "female brains" are overly simplistic.

This challenges neuro sexism—the tendency to attribute ability or behaviour to biological sex alone.

Chapter 2:
The Hormonal Influence

Chapter Goal

- To explore how hormones like testosterone, estrogen, and oxytocin influence human behaviour—and to clear up common myths about how they affect gender, emotion, and cognition. This chapter emphasizes that hormones affect everyone, just in different patterns and contexts.

Chapter 2: The Hormonal Influence

- Testosterone, estrogen, oxytocin
- Hormones and behaviour
- Impact of menstrual cycle, puberty, and menopause

Section 1: Testosterone, estrogen, oxytocin

- Testosterone – Often linked to dominance, aggression, and spatial abilities, but also plays a role in motivation and confidence in all genders.
- Commonly associated with aggression, competition, and risk-taking, but its role is more complex.
- Present in both men and women, though typically at higher levels in men.
- Influences muscle mass, libido, and certain cognitive traits (e.g., spatial abilities), but its behavioural effects are context-dependent.

- In some studies, testosterone increases pro-social behaviour when social reputation is at stake—showing it doesn't always fuel aggression.
- Estrogen Associated with mood regulation, memory, and social sensitivity. Levels fluctuate significantly in females during the menstrual cycle
- Key in regulating the female reproductive system, but also supports brain function, including memory, verbal fluency, and emotion regulation.
- Estrogen receptors are found throughout the brain—especially in the hippocampus and prefrontal cortex.
- In both sexes, estrogen helps maintain neural plasticity and mood stability.
- Oxytocin – Known as the "bonding hormone," it supports social connection, trust, and empathy. Active in both sexes, especially during childbirth, sex, and caregiving.
- Often called the "bonding hormone" or "love hormone."
- Plays a role in attachment, trust, and social bonding, particularly during childbirth, breastfeeding, and sexual activity.
- Elevated in parents of all genders and in people engaged in caregiving or emotional support.
- Effects of oxytocin also depend on context: in some cases, it increases in-group bonding but can intensify distrust toward outsiders

Section 2: Hormones and Behaviour:

- Hormones influence behaviour, but not in isolation. Their effects depend on context, environment, and individual differences.
- For example, testosterone may enhance risk-taking in competitive situations, but not across the board.
- Estrogen may improve verbal memory, but other factors (e.g., stress, sleep) also play key roles.
- Hormones influence, but do not determine, behaviour.
- Their effects are shaped by:
    - Receptor sensitivity (some people are more responsive).
    - Social environment (e.g., testosterone may enhance competition more in competitive settings).
    - Experience and learning (e.g., exposure to nurturing roles can modulate oxytocin release).
- The interaction between hormones and the brain is bidirectional: your behaviour and emotions can also influence hormone levels.

Life Stages and Hormonal Shifts:

- Menstrual cycle: Estrogen and progesterone levels shift across the cycle, sometimes affecting mood, energy, and cognition. These effects vary widely among individuals.

- Puberty: A major hormonal surge restructures brain development, often exaggerating gendered behaviour—but experience and environment still matter greatly.
- Menopause: Estrogen levels decline, which can influence mood, memory, and sleep—but many women adapt well, and cognitive decline is not inevitable.

Section 3: Impact of menstrual cycle, puberty, and menopause

- 1. Menstrual Cycle
- The menstrual cycle is a monthly hormonal cycle that prepares the body for pregnancy. It typically lasts around 28 days and is regulated by several hormones.

Key Hormones:

- Estrogen – promotes growth of the uterine lining and regulates mood
- Progesterone – stabilizes the uterine lining, impacts mood and appetite
- FSH (Follicle-Stimulating Hormone) – stimulates egg development
- LH (Luteinizing Hormone) – triggers ovulation

Hormonal Influence:

- Mood swings due to estrogen and progesterone fluctuations
- Bloating, fatigue, breast tenderness
- Increased/decreased libido
- Premenstrual Syndrome (PMS) and, in more severe cases, Premenstrual Dysphoric Disorder (PMDD)
- 2.Puberty
- it is the transition from childhood to sexual maturity, typically starting between ages 8–13 for girls and 9–14 for boys.

Key Hormones:

- GnRH (Gonadotropin-Releasing Hormone) - triggers puberty
- Estrogen in girls - drives breast development, menstruation, and body fat distribution
- Testosterone in boys - drives muscle growth, voice changes, and facial hair

Hormonal Influence:

- Rapid physical growth (growth spurts)
- Development of secondary sexual characteristics
- Emotional shifts, moodiness, and heightened sensitivity or aggression
- Body image and identity development often influenced by hormonal and physical changes

3. Menopause

it is typically occurs between ages 45–55 and marks the end of menstruation and fertility. It is defined as 12 months without a period.

Key Hormonal Changes:

- Estrogen and progesterone levels drop significantly
- FSH levels increase as the body tries to stimulate the ovaries

Hormonal Influence:

- Hot flashes and night sweats
- Mood changes, anxiety, and irritability
- Sleep disturbances
- Vaginal dryness and changes in libido
- Increased risk of osteoporosis and heart disease due to low estrogen

Summary Table:

Phase	Key Hormones	Main Effects
Menstrual Cycle	Estragen, Progesterone, FSH, LH	Mood changes, PMS, cramps, energy shifts
Puberty	Estragen (girls), Testosterone (boys), GnRH	Growth, emotional shifts, sexual development
Menopause	↓ Estragen, ↓ Progesterone, ↑ FSH	Hot flashes, mood swings, insomnia, long-term health changes

Chapter 3: Evolutionary Psychology and Survival Thinking

Chapter Goal

To explore how evolutionary forces have shaped gender roles, behaviours, and cognitive patterns—while also highlighting the limitations and debates around evolutionary psychology.

Evolutionary Psychology and Survival Thinking

- Gender roles in evolution
- Risk-taking and aggression
- Empathy and caregiving

Evolutionary psychology seeks to explain human behaviour through the lens of natural selection. Traits that improved our ancestors' chances of survival and reproduction became embedded in our psychology. This chapter explores how gender roles, risk-taking, aggression, empathy, and caregiving evolved as adaptive strategies in our ancestral environment. While cultural evolution and modern society have challenged and reshaped these roles, their evolutionary roots still influence behaviour.

Section 1: Gender Roles in Evolution

Evolutionary pressures shaped different survival strategies for males and females due to their distinct reproductive roles. Historically, males increased reproductive success through competition and access to multiple partners, which favoured traits such as strength, dominance, and status-seeking. Females, by contrast, invested more heavily in offspring through pregnancy, nursing, and caregiving. This favoured traits like selectivity in mates, social bonding, and nurturing.

These pressures laid the foundation for gender-specific tendencies:

- Males: More likely to take risks, engage in physical competition, and prioritize status.
- Females: More inclined toward nurturing roles, social cohesion, and emotional intelligence.
- Evolutionary psychology proposes that many differences in male and female behaviour stem from distinct reproductive challenges.
- Males and females evolved different strategies due to reproductive roles.
- Females: More nurturing and selective in choosing partners to ensure offspring survival.
- These tendencies helped early humans survive but are influenced today by culture and social change.

Reproductive Investment Theory

According to Robert Trivers Parental Investment Theory, females have a higher obligatory investment in offspring (pregnancy, childbirth, breastfeeding), while males have the potential to reproduce with minimal biological cost. This difference led to:

- Female selectivity in mate choice, prioritizing traits like resource availability, protection, and long-term commitment.
- Male competitiveness, with an emphasis on acquiring status, strength, and access to fertile mates.

Hunter-Gatherer Division of Labour

In ancestral hunter-gatherer societies:

- Men often hunted, which required spatial awareness, tool use, and cooperative strategy.
- Women gathered plant-based food and cared for children, fostering social intelligence and multitasking abilities.
- This division wasn't rigid but helped shape modern sex differences in cognitive styles and behaviour patterns.

Modern Manifestations

- While modern society has transformed gender roles through culture and technology:
- Evolutionary legacies persist in some behaviours: men are more likely to prioritize physical attractiveness in partners; women more often value social stability and financial resources.
- Importantly, these are tendencies, not rules—individual variation and cultural factors play major roles.

Section 2: Risk-Taking and Aggression

In ancestral environments, risk-taking could yield high rewards—such as securing food, mates, or territory. However, it also came with dangers. Evolution favoured calculated risk-taking in contexts that boosted reproductive success. Risk-taking and aggression were often adaptive in ancestral environments. They helped individuals secure food, territory, and mates—but carried significant danger.

- Aggression, particularly in males, was a strategy for dominance and mate competition. Hormones like testosterone reinforced this tendency.
- Young males typically show the highest rates of risk-taking, aligning with periods of peak mating interest.
- Intrasexual competition (especially among males) led to aggressive behaviours to establish dominance hierarchies.
- Physical aggression was often a means to resolve disputes or claim status within a group.
- Testosterone is linked to increased aggression and dominance behaviours, particularly during reproductive prime (ages 15–30).
- Modern environments differ drastically from the ancestral world, yet these evolved behaviours persist—often manifesting in areas like sports, entrepreneurship, or even crime.
- Males, especially in early adulthood, often engage in risky behaviours (e.g., fighting, dangerous sports, extreme driving).

- From an evolutionary lens, risk-taking can increase status or access to mates, even if it reduces lifespan.
- Aggression evolved mainly in males for competition over mates and resources.
- Risk-taking behaviour helped secure status or food but came with dangers.
- Today, these traits show up in things like extreme sports, business ventures, or crime—but aren't always adaptive.
- However, in modern settings, these behaviours can be maladaptive—leading to accidents, incarceration, or health problems. Evolution didn't "anticipate" the complexity of modern society.
- 3. Empathy and Caregiving

While aggression and competition were important, cooperation and caregiving were essential for human survival—especially because humans have long childhoods and complex social structures in contrast to aggression and risk-taking, empathy and caregiving evolved to support social bonding, group cohesion, and offspring survival. These traits were crucial in small, interdependent groups where cooperation meant better chances of survival.

While caregiving roles were historically more pronounced in women due to biological constraints, both sexes evolved capacities for empathy and nurturing—vital for maintaining social bonds and group stability.

Section 3: The Role of Empathy

- Empathy enabled understanding others' emotions and needs, which fostered trust and mutual aid.
- Caregiving behaviours, especially in mothers, ensured the survival of vulnerable infants. These behaviours are often hormonally influenced (e.g., oxytocin) and socially reinforced.
- Empathy evolved to enhance social cohesion, improve conflict resolution, and facilitate cooperation.
- Brain regions like the anterior cingulate cortex and mirror neuron systems are involved in empathetic responses.
- Empathy allows individuals to predict and respond to the emotional states of others, which increases trust and strengthens bonds.
- Empathy evolved to strengthen group bonds and cooperation.
- Caregiving behaviours ensured the survival of young, especially by mothers.
- Traits like compassion and social support are key to human group survival

Caregiving and Attachment

- Infant dependency required prolonged caregiving, favouring traits that promote nurturing behaviours.

- Oxytocin, a hormone associated with bonding, is released during caregiving activities (e.g., breastfeeding, hugging), reinforcing attachment.
- Attachment theory (Bowlby & Ainsworth) suggests that early bonding styles influence adult relationships.

While caregiving was traditionally associated with females, all Parenting (shared caregiving among group members) was common in human evolution—suggesting caregiving capacity evolved in both sexes.

Part II: Psychological Warfare

Chapter 4: Emotions and Empathy

- Emotional expression differences
- Emotional intelligence in men vs. women
- Cultural expectations on feelings

Chapter 5: Communication Combat

- Language use in men and women
- Interruptions, tone, and intent
- Listening vs. problem-solving
- Workplace communication

Chapter 6: Decision-Making and Risk

- Logic vs. intuition
- How stress affects decision-making

Brain scans in risk analysis**Part II: Psychological Warfare**

Chapter 4: Emotions and Empathy

- Emotional expression differences
- Emotional intelligence in men vs. women
- Cultural expectations on feelings

Section 1: Emotional Expression Differences (Men vs. Women)

General Patterns:

- Women are often seen as more expressive with their emotions. This can be attributed to both biological factors (like hormonal differences) and socialization (how society teaches us to behave). For example, women might be more likely to openly express feelings such as sadness, joy, or anxiety, and they may use verbal and non-verbal cues (like facial expressions or body language) to communicate those emotions.
    - Example: When women are upset, they might talk through their emotions, seek validation, or share their feelings with others. They may show facial expressions like crying or frowning that reflect what they're experiencing internally.
- Men, traditionally, are expected to maintain a more stoic or restrained emotional demeanour. This stems from societal expectations around masculinity, where showing vulnerability or certain emotions (like fear or

sadness) is sometimes seen as a weakness. Anger, frustration, or competitiveness, however, are more socially accepted expressions for men.

   - Example: Men may show frustration through physical actions (like slamming a door or raising their voice), or they might suppress feelings of sadness or fear, which can sometimes lead to emotional bottling up. They may also channel these emotions into action—whether that's through problem-solving or taking on tasks to regain control of the situation.

Why the Difference?

- Biological influences: Hormones like oestrogen (higher in women) and testosterone (higher in men) impact how emotions are experienced and expressed. Estragon is linked to higher emotional reactivity, while testosterone is associated with more reserved emotional expression.
- Socialization: From an early age, boys and girls are taught to express their emotions differently. Girls are often encouraged to share and connect emotionally, while boys are taught to "toughen up" and suppress certain feelings. This social training is reinforced in various settings—family dynamics, schools, media, etc.

1. Frequency and Intensity of Emotional Expression

- Women: Tend to express emotions more frequently and intensely, especially emotions like sadness, fear, and joy.

- Men: Are more likely to express anger and less likely to show vulnerability-related emotions (e.g., sadness or fear).

2. Nonverbal Expression

- Women: Use more facial expressions, gestures, and vocal cues to convey emotions.
- Men: Tend to use less expressive body language and facial cues, often suppressing emotional displays.

3. Socialization and Gender Norms

- Women are generally socialized to be nurturing, emotionally expressive, and relationship-oriented.
- Men are often taught to value stoicism, independence, and emotional restraint–especially in Western cultures.

4. Biological and Neurological Factors

- Hormones like testosterone and oxytocin may influence emotional regulation and empathy levels.
- Brain studies show some structural and functional differences in regions associated with emotion processing (e.g., the amygdala and prefrontal cortex), though interpretations vary.

5. Cultural Influences

- In individualistic cultures (e.g., the U.S.), emotional expression is more accepted overall but still gendered.

- In collectivistic cultures, emotional restraint may be expected for both genders but still differs by role expectations.

6. Emotional Recognition

- Women are generally better at recognizing and interpreting others' emotions, possibly due to both evolutionary and socialization influences.

7. Emotional Regulation

- Men may use distraction or suppression more often as emotional regulation strategies.

Women may seek social support and ruminate more, which can both help and hinder emotional regulation.**Summary**

Category	Women	Men
Frequency of Expression	Higher	Lower
Typical Emotions Shown	Sadness, fear, happiness, empathy	Anger, pride
Nonverbal Expression	More expressive	More reserved
Social Expectations	Encouraged to express emotions	Encouraged to suppress emotions
Emotion Recognition	More accurate	Less accurate
Regulation Style	Social support, rumination	Suppression, distraction

Section 2. Emotional Intelligence in Men vs. Women

Emotional Intelligence (EQ):

- Emotional Intelligence refers to the ability to recognize, understand, manage, and influence emotions in oneself and others. It includes skills like emotional awareness, empathy, self-regulation, and social awareness.

Research shows that:

- Women tend to score higher than men on empathy (understanding others' emotions) and social awareness (sensing emotional dynamics in relationships). This may be because women are socialized to be more attuned to emotional cues and prioritize relationship-building.
    - Example: Women might be quicker to recognize when a friend is upset or offer support when someone is going through a tough time.
- Men, however, tend to score higher on self-regulation and emotional management, particularly in situations of stress or high pressure. They might also be better at using their emotional awareness to solve problems or take action. This is particularly true in settings where logical decision-making is valued over emotional expression.
    - Example: Men might focus more on "fixing" a problem when someone is upset rather

than engaging in an emotional conversation about the issue, because their emotional intelligence might emphasize action over emotional expression.

Why These Differences?

- Biology and Hormones: The difference in testosterone and estrogen impacts how emotions are processed and expressed. Estrogen can make women more emotionally sensitive, while testosterone may make men more focused on action and less concerned with emotional dialogue.
- Social Expectations: From a young age, boys are often taught to be emotionally "strong" or "resilient," which may prevent them from developing the same depth of empathy as girls, who are socialized to be more nurturing and emotionally open.

Section 3: Cultural Expectations on Feelings (and Gender Norms)

Cultural Influence:

- Gender norms around emotions are deeply embedded in cultural expectations. Most cultures place different emotional expectations on men and women. Women are often encouraged to express emotions openly, while men are pressured to remain controlled or even indifferent, especially when dealing with "negative" emotions.

Examples of Cultural Norms:

- In many societies, anger is viewed as acceptable for men, but sadness or vulnerability is less acceptable. Women, on the other hand, might be expected to show compassion, nurturance, and empathy, and may be encouraged to express their emotions verbally.
- Men: The idea that men should be "tough" or "stoic" often comes from traditional ideas of masculinity (sometimes called the "man-up" mentality). Men who express fear, sadness, or even anxiety might be viewed as less masculine. This pressure is increasingly being challenged in modern societies, with more men embracing emotional vulnerability, but it's still a dominant cultural influence.
- Women: Women, conversely, are often seen as the emotional caregivers or nurturers. There's pressure for women to be more emotionally available, which can be both a positive and a negative thing. While being nurturing is celebrated, women can also be stereotyped as overly emotional or "too sensitive" when they express strong feelings. The line between empathy and emotional over-engagement can sometimes be blurry.

Cultural Expectations and Emotional Suppression:

- Men in many cultures may feel the need to suppress emotions that are viewed as "weak," particularly sadness and fear. This can lead to emotional suppression, which over time can result in mental health challenges, including depression and anxiety.

- Women might experience the opposite. While their emotional expression is often more socially accepted, there's a pressure to balance empathy with maintaining their own emotional boundaries. This can sometimes lead to emotional burnout or an overemphasis on the needs of others at the expense of self-care.

Chapter 5: Communication Combat

- Language use in men and women
- Interruptions, tone, and intent
- Listening vs. problem-solving
- Workplace communication

Section 1: Language Use in Men vs. Women

1. General Patterns:

- Women typically use language as a tool for connection and relationship-building. They might focus more on empathy, emotion, and expressing feelings in their conversations. Women often use language to seek validation, share personal experiences, and maintain emotional bonds.
- Their speech often reflects a desire for connection, understanding, and cooperation. in a conversation, a woman might say, "*I know how you feel,*" to express empathy and maintain closeness.
    - Example: A conversation between two women may involve a lot of emotional exchange, validation, and sharing personal details to establish a deeper connection.
- Men, on the other hand, are often socialized to use language as a tool for asserting independence, status,

or solving problems. Men may use language to convey information, achieve goals, or compete rather than to bond emotionally. Their conversations can be more direct or task-oriented.

- Men, by contrast, are more likely to use language for exchanging information, asserting opinions, or achieving a goal. In male conversations, the emphasis is often on problem-solving rather than emotional expression. For instance, a man may respond to someone sharing a problem by offering a solution rather than emotional support.
    - Example: Men might talk more about facts or ideas and less about personal feelings or emotional experiences, especially in casual settings.

2. Conversational Style

Women often engage in what linguists call a collaborative or cooperative style, while men tend to exhibit a more competitive or independent style.

- Women frequently use inclusive language, such as *"we"* or *"let's,"* and are more likely to ask questions that invite input. They tend to use gestures like nodding, and phrases like *"you know?"* or *"right?"* to seek affirmation and create a sense of shared understanding.
- Men, in contrast, may be more direct and assertive. They often interrupt more frequently (especially in mixed-gender groups), and use language to establish

dominance or status in a group. Men are less likely to use backchanneling cues like *"mm-hmm"* or *"I see."* When telling stories, they tend to focus on action and outcomes, rather than emotion or character.

3. Emotional Expression

Gender roles heavily influence how men and women express emotion through language.

- Women's language is generally more emotionally expressive. They use a wider emotional vocabulary and are more comfortable discussing feelings openly. This expressiveness is encouraged from a young age in many cultures, where girls are praised for being sensitive and nurturing.
- Men, however, are often taught to suppress or control emotional expression, especially in public. Their language may focus more on facts and logic, and they may avoid openly discussing vulnerability, instead expressing emotions like anger or frustration more readily than sadness or fear.

4. Word Choice and Style

- Women tend to use more adjectives, especially those that are emotive or evaluative, such as *"lovely,"* *"adorable,"* or *"wonderful."* Their speech may also include hedging phrases like *"I think,"* *"maybe,"* or *"kind of,"* which can make their language seem more polite or less assertive.
- Men's language is often more straightforward and less hedged. They may use fewer modifiers and more

commands or declarative statements. This can make their speech seem more confident or authoritative, though sometimes less diplomatic.

5. Use of Apologies and Politeness

Women are generally more likely to apologize, not necessarily because they are always at fault, but because they use apologies to smooth over interactions and maintain harmony. For example, a woman might say, *"I'm sorry, but can I ask a question?"* even when she hasn't done anything wrong.

Men, on the other hand, apologize less frequently, as doing so can be seen (socially or psychologically) as a loss of status or power. Their speech is typically more direct, which can be perceived as confidence or, in some cases, as brusqueness.

6. Storytelling Differences

Men and women also tend to differ in how they tell stories:

- Women's stories often focus on relationships, emotions, and context. They may include detailed descriptions and multiple perspectives. A story from a woman might centre on how people felt or how events affected others emotionally.
- Men's stories are often goal-oriented and focus on achievement, action, or humour. A typical male narrative might involve overcoming a challenge, being clever, or winning a competition – with less emphasis on how everyone felt.

Section 2: Interruptions, Tone, and Intent

Interruptions: How They Happen and What They Mean

Interruptions reflect how men and women engage differently – one more competitively, the other more cooperatively. Interruptions are a natural part of conversation, but they can carry very different meanings depending on who's doing the interrupting and why

- When women interrupt, it's often to show support or engagement.
- For example, they might say "Right!" or "Exactly!" while someone else is talking – not to take over, but to show they're actively listening. This is called a cooperative interruption and is common in female communication styles, where the focus is often on relationship-building.
- When men interrupt, it is more often to take the conversational floor – for example, to add their opinion, correct something, or shift the topic. These are known as competitive interruptions. This reflects a style of communication that often values assertiveness and control of the discussion.

That said, context matters. A man may interrupt supportively, and a woman may interrupt competitively – but on average, this gendered pattern holds, especially in public or mixed-gender conversations.

Tone: What It Sounds Like and How It's Perceived

- Tone refers to how something is said – the emotion, pitch, and rhythm behind the words. Tone reveals emotional expression and social intent – more varied and relational in women, more restrained and assertive in men.

- Women's tone is often more expressive and emotionally nuanced. They tend to vary pitch more, use a rising intonation (even in statements), and soften their voice in emotionally sensitive situations. This kind of tone can convey warmth, openness, and empathy. However, in some contexts (like the workplace), a rising tone might be misinterpreted as uncertainty or lack of confidence.
- Men's tone is usually more monotone and firmer, especially in formal settings. This can come across as strong, confident, or authoritative. But in emotional situations, the same tone may be seen as cold or unfeeling. This is partly due to social expectations that men should speak with control and minimal emotional expression.

Tone isn't just about voice – it's about how others interpret emotional intent. People may judge the same tone differently depending on the speaker's gender, even if the content is identical.

Intent: Why People Speak the Way They Do

Intent refers to the purpose behind a person's words – what they're trying to achieve through speech.

Intent **drives communication style – often focused on connection for women, and control or clarity for men.**

- Women often speak with the intent to build connection and avoid conflict. Their speech tends to be more collaborative and indirect. For example, instead of saying "That's wrong," a woman might say, "I'm not sure that's quite right – what do you think?"

This approach is more about keeping the social atmosphere comfortable than asserting dominance.

- Men, in contrast, often speak with the intent to deliver information, solve a problem, or assert a point. Their language can be more direct and task-oriented. A man might say, "That won't work. Here's why," focusing on the solution rather than how it might be received emotionally

These differing intentions can lead to miscommunication. A woman might feel a man is being too blunt, while a man might think a woman is being vague or avoiding the point – even though neither is wrong, just operating with different conversational goals.

These patterns are not absolute – many men and women break them depending on context, personality, or culture. But being aware of these tendencies can help us become better communicators and more empathetic listeners, especially in mixed-gender conversations.

Section 3: Listening vs. Problem-Solving

In conversations between women and men, one of the most common misunderstandings arises from how each approaches emotional expression and support. Often, women want to talk to feel understood, while men feel a need to offer solutions. This mismatch can cause both sides to feel frustrated, dismissed, or disconnected–even when both parties have good intentions.

- Women tend to value listening as an important part of communication. They often want to share and process emotions, seeking empathy and understanding from the other person. They might not necessarily be looking for solutions but rather for someone to hear and validate their feelings.

  - Example: A woman talks about a stressful day at work, and she wants a friend or partner to listen, express sympathy, and acknowledge her feelings.

- Men, however, are often socialized to approach conversation with a problem-solving mindset. When someone shares a problem with them, their instinct is often to jump into action mode—offering solutions, advice, or ways to fix the issue.
  - Example: A man listens to the same conversation about a stressful day at work and immediately offers advice or suggestions to "fix" the problem, even if the woman wasn't seeking that kind of help.

The Misunderstanding:

- This difference often leads to frustration. Women may feel that men aren't being empathetic or attentive, while men may feel that their solutions aren't appreciated. In reality, the issue may just be that women are looking for emotional support, while men are trying to solve the problem.

1. Social Conditioning: How We're Taught to Communicate

- Women are often socialized to value emotional connection, verbal sharing, and empathy. Talking about feelings isn't necessarily about fixing a problem–it's about bonding and processing.

- Men are often conditioned to focus on action, results, and fixing. Listening without doing something may feel passive or unhelpful.

This isn't about biology–it's about learned behaviour. Men and women can both learn to be good listeners or problem-solvers, but culture often pushes them toward different styles.

2. The Common Scenario

A woman says: "Work is driving me crazy. My boss keeps piling on more projects." A man responds: "Then just say no. Or start looking for a new job." This seems helpful, but it often leads to frustration. Why?

- The woman may feel unheard–she wasn't asking for a solution, just to be understood.
- The man may feel confused–he offered help and now she's upset.

What she might have needed instead:

"That sounds really stressful. Want to talk more about it?"

3. What's Really Happening

- Women often talk to process. It helps them clarify their own feelings and build closeness.
- Men often listen to respond. They want to be useful–so they offer solutions.

Neither is wrong–but they're mismatched when the goal is emotional connection vs. practical advice.

4. How to Bridge the Gap

For Men:

- Pause before offering advice. Ask:
  "Do you want me to just listen, or are you looking for solutions?"
- Focus on emotional validation first:
  "That really sucks. I can see why you're frustrated."
- Understand that your presence is often more powerful than your advice.

For Women:

- Be clear about what you need:
  "I don't need you to fix this–I just need to vent."
- Recognize that many men feel love by trying to "help" through action.
- If you do want solutions, say so explicitly to avoid mixed signals.

5. In Relationships: Emotional Safety vs. Performance Pressure

- Women often want emotional presence. Feeling heard creates intimacy.
- Men often feel pressure to "get it right" or "fix it fast." If they can't solve the problem, they may feel inadequate.

This creates a disconnect:

She wants connection → He offers solutions → She feels dismissed → He feels unappreciated.

The fix? Empathy first. Problem-solving second—if invited.

6. Final Thought: Listening ***Is*** Helping

For many women, the most powerful form of support is feeling emotionally seen for many men, the most meaningful way to show love is by doing something useful. When both people recognize these instincts, they can learn to meet in the middle:

- Men can learn to slow down and listen first.
- Women can learn to communicate their needs clearly.

"I don't need you to fix this—I just need you to be here with me." That one sentence can change everything.

Section 4: Workplace Communication

Gender and Power Dynamics:

- Workplace communication can be especially complex because of gender norms and power dynamics. Women may face challenges when trying to assert authority in environments that reward directness and dominance, which are often associated with male communication styles.
    - Example: Women in leadership positions may be perceived as too soft or indecisive if they adopt a more collaborative or empathetic tone. On the other hand, when they are direct or assertive, they may be labelled as **bossy** or too aggressive.

- Men might face less pushback when they adopt more dominant or task-oriented communication styles. However, they might also struggle with emotional intelligence in the workplace, as they're less likely to engage in the empathy or listening that creates strong relationships.

Barriers to Effective Communication in the Workplace:

- Interruptions can be particularly problematic in meetings. Studies show that men interrupt more often than women, which can undermine women's voices in professional settings and lead to misalignment in how ideas are presented and valued.
    - Example: In a brainstorming session, men might dominate the conversation, and women may hesitate to interrupt or assert themselves, even if they have valuable input.

Tone can be an issue in both performance reviews and team communication. Women's softer tones may be seen as less authoritative by others, and men's blunt tones might be perceived as aggressive or disruptive.

Chapter 6: Decision-Making and Risk

- Logic vs. intuition
- How stress affects decision-making
- Brain scans in risk analysis

Section 1: Logic vs. Intuition in Decision-Making

Logic-Based Decision-Making:

- Logical decision-making is based on rational thinking and systematic analysis. It involves evaluating facts, considering potential outcomes, weighing pros and cons, and using data to make a choice. This approach relies on the prefrontal cortex (the part of the brain associated with planning, reasoning, and decision-making).
  - Example: Deciding on a new job might involve weighing the salary, benefits, career advancement potential, and work-life balance. You might make a spreadsheet or list to compare options before making your decision.
- Advantages: It is typically methodical, objective, and avoids impulsive decisions. Logical thinkers often prefer structured environments and may feel more comfortable with quantifiable data.

Intuitive Decision-Making:

- Intuition involves relying on gut feelings, instincts, or unconscious knowledge. It's a fast, automatic form of decision-making where you rely on patterns and past experiences, rather than consciously analysing information. Intuitive decisions are often quick, without the need for deep analysis.
    - Example: If you've had a good experience working with someone in the past, you might intuitively trust them with a new project without needing to weigh all the details. Or, choosing between two restaurants—one might "feel" like the better option, even if there's no clear data to support it.
- Advantages: Intuitive decisions can be faster and more fluid, especially in situations where quick choices are needed (like emergencies or social interactions). It's often guided by subconscious experience and emotional intelligence, which can sometimes give better results in ambiguous or high-pressure situations.

Logic vs. Intuition:

- Complementary Approaches: While logic is powerful in complex, well-defined situations, intuition often shines when there's uncertainty or a need for quick action. In fact, research suggests that intuitive thinking can be enhanced by experience, making it a reliable tool when it aligns with expertise.

- The Caveat: Over-relying on intuition without logical checks can lead to biases and errors in judgment (e.g., the availability bias, where we base decisions on what is most readily available or memorable, rather than the full picture). On the flip side, over-relying on logic can lead to paralysis by analysis, where overthinking prevents action.

Section 2: How Stress Affects Decision-Making

Stress has a profound effect on how we make decisions. Under stress, emotions and physiological changes can significantly alter our decision-making process. Here's how:

Stress and Cognitive Function:

- Under high levels of stress, the body releases stress hormones like cortisol, which can affect brain regions associated with logical thinking, planning, and impulse control (such as the prefrontal cortex).
    - Short-Term Stress: In situations of acute stress (like a deadline or emergency), you might make faster decisions, but those choices may be more impulsive or short-term oriented.
    - Chronic Stress: Over time, chronic stress can impair the working memory and attention, which affects your ability to make thoughtful, clear-headed decisions.

Fight or Flight Response:

- When we perceive stress (especially life-threatening stress), the amygdala (the brain's emotional canter) takes over, triggering the fight or flight response. This prioritizes immediate survival and often results in more emotion-driven decisions rather than logical analysis.
    - Example: In a high-stress situation, you might overreact, act impulsively, or make a decision that feels safer in the moment (e.g., avoiding risk) but may not be optimal in the long term.

Stress and Risk-Taking:

- Interestingly, stress can also increase risk-taking behaviour in some individuals. In situations of stress, people might become more risk-seeking, especially if they feel they have nothing to lose (a phenomenon known as the "loss aversion" bias).
    - Example: Someone might take financial risks (like gambling or investing in speculative stocks) when feeling stressed, trying to compensate for perceived losses or frustrations.

Stress Reduction and Better Decisions:

- Techniques like mindfulness, breathing exercises, and relaxation strategies can reduce the effects of stress and help people return to a more balanced decision-making state. Studies have shown that calm individuals are better at evaluating risks and making rational choices.

Section 3: Brain Scans in Risk Analysis

Neuroscience of Decision-Making:

- Neuroscience has made great strides in understanding how our brains make decisions—especially when it comes to risk. Brain scans (like MRI and EEG) have shown that certain brain regions are heavily involved in risk assessment and decision-making.

Key Brain Regions Involved:

- Prefrontal Cortex (PFC): The PFC is the brain's decision-making hub, responsible for logical reasoning, planning, and impulse control. This area is most active during complex decision-making processes, especially when the outcomes are uncertain or risky.
    - Example: When deciding whether to take a financial risk (e.g., investing in the stock market), the PFC helps you evaluate potential gains and losses, while also considering the long-term consequences.
- Amygdala: The amygdala, part of the limbic system, is the emotional canter of the brain, responsible for processing fear and other emotions. In risky situations, it can trigger the fight-or-flight response, which may lead to emotionally driven decisions.
    - Example: In a dangerous situation, the amygdala may dominate, urging you to avoid

risk or retreat, even if the logical analysis suggests otherwise.

- Striatum: The striatum is associated with reward processing and anticipating pleasure. This region lights up when you're considering decisions that might lead to positive outcomes, like the possibility of winning a gamble or getting a promotion. It's also implicated in the tendency to take risks in pursuit of rewards.

Risk-Taking and Brain Activity:

- Brain scans show that risk-taking behaviour is linked to increased activity in the dopaminergic pathways, which are responsible for feelings of pleasure and reward. These pathways are often more active in individuals who are predisposed to risky behaviour.
- When individuals are presented with risky options, the balance between the prefrontal cortex (rational) and amygdala (emotional) activity determines whether they will make a risky or safe choice.

Brain Scans and Biases:

- Brain scans also reveal that biases like overconfidence or loss aversion—affect our decision-making. For example, when people experience loss aversion, areas of the brain associated with fear and regret light up, making them more likely to avoid risky decisions.

Part III: The Social Arena

Chapter 7: Nature vs. Nurture Revisited

- Gender roles through upbringing
- Media, toys, and school systems
- How societal norms shape thought

Chapter 8: The Workplace Mind Divide

- Gender bias in leadership
- Multitasking vs. focus
- Emotional labour in teams

Chapter 9: Relationships and Love Languages

- How men and women express love
- Conflict resolution styles
- Sex, intimacy, and communication

Chapter 10: Finding Common Ground

- Embracing differences without division
- Communication strategies
- How to use knowledge for harmony

Chapter 7: Nature vs. Nurture Revisited

- Gender roles through upbringing
- Media, toys, and school systems
- How societal norms shape thought

Section 1: Gender Roles Through Upbringing

How Families Influence Gender Roles:

- Parenting Styles: From an early age, parents start teaching children what is considered appropriate behaviour for their gender. This often happens through both direct instruction (e.g., "boys don't cry" or "girls are nurturing") and modelling behaviour (e.g., how fathers and mothers interact in their relationships).
    - Example: Parents may encourage their sons to engage in active or competitive activities (e.g., sports) and daughters to be more nurturing or passive (e.g., playing with dolls or caring for younger siblings).
- Gendered Expectations: Parents may unconsciously reinforce gendered expectations through their language. For example, praising a boy for being brave when they face something difficult, while praising a girl for being quiet or obedient. Over time, this reinforces the idea that certain traits (like aggression

or competitiveness) are associated with men, while others (like empathy or cooperation) are linked to women.

- Toys and Activities: The types of toys children are given and the activities they're encouraged to pursue are heavily gendered. Boys are often given toys that promote building, action, and competition (e.g., Legos, action figures), while girls are given toys that emphasize caregiving, beauty, and domesticity (e.g., dolls, kitchen sets).
    - Example: A boy might be encouraged to play with construction sets that help develop problem-solving skills, while a girl may be given dolls that focus more on relational and emotional skills.

The Long-Term Impact of Upbringing:

These early experiences significantly influence how children internalize and express their gender identity. In the long term, children raised in environments where gender roles are rigidly defined may struggle with gender non-conformity or feel confined by their assigned roles. Conversely, children raised in environments that encourage flexibility around gender may grow up with more fluid or inclusive understandings of gender.

Section 2: Media, Toys, and School Systems

Media and Gender Representation:

- The media (TV shows, movies, advertisements, social media) plays a massive role in reinforcing and shaping gender roles. From childhood onward, the media often promotes certain gender stereotypes through characters and narratives.

  - Example: In many popular cartoons or movies, male characters are often depicted as action heroes, leaders, or adventurers, while female characters are shown as caregivers, romantic interests, or supporting roles. This gender bifurcation can reinforce the idea that men are meant to lead and act, while women should care and nurture.

- Representation in Advertising: Advertisements are particularly powerful in shaping gender expectations. Commercials often target men and women with gender-specific messaging, reinforcing ideas like men being strong, independent, and dominant, while women are nurturing, caring, and focused on appearance.

  - Example: A car commercial might depict men driving a high-performance vehicle through rough terrain, while a cleaning product commercial might depict women cleaning with a product that promises to make their homes look perfect.

Toys and Gender Socialization:

- Toys are one of the earliest places where children learn gender norms. They are often divided into "boys' toys" and "girls' toys", which promotes the idea that certain activities are appropriate only for certain genders.

    - Example: Action figures or cars are marketed heavily toward boys, while dolls or kitchen sets are geared toward girls. This division reinforces stereotypes like assertion and dominance for boys, and domesticity and nurturing for girls.

- The Pink-Blue Divide: The color-coding of toys (pink for girls, blue for boys) is another tool of socialization. It sends the message that gendered preferences are natural and immutable, even from birth. These color-coded toys are often accompanied by narratives that suggest girls should focus on appearance and domestic skills, while boys should focus on action and independence.
- Gender-neutral Toys: Recently, there's been a shift toward gender-neutral toys (e.g., gender-neutral building blocks or dolls). However, despite some progress, many toy manufacturers continue to use traditional gender-marketing strategies.

School Systems and Gender:

- Schools play a major role in shaping gender roles, from how students are grouped, to the subjects they are encouraged to pursue, and the ways teachers interact with boys and girls.
    - Example: Teachers may unintentionally praise boys for assertiveness or leadership, while girls are praised for being well-behaved

or quiet. Boys are often encouraged to pursue STEM (science, technology, engineering, and math) subjects, while girls are pushed toward the humanities or arts.

- Gendered Socialization in Classrooms: In many classrooms, boys and girls are expected to behave in gender-conforming ways. Boys might be reprimanded for being too emotional, while girls may be punished for being too assertive or outspoken.
- This reinforces traditional gender norms of emotional restraint in boys and passivity in girls.
- Curriculum and Gender: The subjects taught in schools can also reinforce gender roles. For instance, history might focus on male leaders and military figures, while literature often centers on female characters in domestic settings or emotional turmoil. In contrast, boys might be encouraged to explore political systems or wars, which further entrenches gendered interests and identities.

Section 3: How Societal Norms Shape Thought

Cultural Narratives and Gender Identity:

- Societal norms are the deeply ingrained expectations about how people should behave, look, or express themselves based on their gender. These norms shape not only how individuals see themselves, but also how they are perceived by others. These cultural scripts often dictate everything from careers and relationships to appearance and personality traits.

- Example: A society may expect men to be assertive, independent, and emotionally controlled, while women may be expected to be nurturing, submissive, and emotionally expressive. These roles can limit personal expression and development, particularly for those who do not fit neatly into the traditional gender categories.

Media and Socialization:

- Media plays a powerful role in shaping these norms. Film, TV, music, and now social media influencers set standards for beauty, behaviour, and success. These representations often reinforce binary gender roles, while also creating unrealistic standards for masculinity and femininity.
  - Example: The ideal male image in media often involves strength, dominance, and stoicism, while the ideal female image is focused on beauty, passivity, and emotionality.

Gender Fluidity and Breaking Norms:

- In recent years, there's been a growing movement toward breaking down rigid gender norms and embracing gender fluidity. People are beginning to challenge the idea that gender must be confined to two categories–male and female–and to recognize a broader spectrum of gender identities and expressions.

- Example: Celebrities, like Harry Styles or Billy Porter, have embraced non-traditional gender expressions, wearing clothing that traditionally belonged to the opposite gender, challenging the norms of masculinity and femininity.
- **Impact of Societal Norms on Thought:**

- Societal norms often create cognitive biases that shape the way people think about themselves and others. For example, the belief that men are naturally more logical and women are more emotional can lead to stereotypes that affect hiring decisions, leadership expectations, and interpersonal relationships.
- These norms can limit personal development and create internal conflicts for individuals who feel pressured to conform to traditional gender roles. For instance, a woman might feel the pressure to be nurturing and caregiving, while also trying to succeed in a male-dominated workplace where competitiveness is valued.

Chapter 8:
The Workplace Mind Divide

- Gender bias in leadership
- Multitasking vs. focus
- Emotional labour in teams

Section 1: Gender Bias in Leadership

The Leadership Gap:

- Despite progress in gender equality, gender bias remains a significant barrier to women's leadership opportunities. Studies consistently show that women face more scrutiny than men in leadership positions, with biases that can shape how their authority, competence, and decisions are perceived.
- Examples of Bias:
    - Double Bind: Women in leadership roles often face a "double bind" where they are expected to exhibit strong leadership traits (assertiveness, confidence, decisiveness) but are criticized for being too aggressive or unlikable if they do. If they choose to display more warmth and empathy, they may be seen as too soft or not strong enough to lead.
    - Stereotypes of Women in Leadership: Women in power may also be viewed

through stereotypes that affect how their decisions are interpreted.

    - For example, if a woman shows emotion in a stressful situation, she might be labelled as irrational, while a man showing the same emotion might be seen as passionate or committed.

- Male-Preferred Leadership Styles: Traditional leadership styles have often been modelled around masculine traits like assertiveness, decisiveness, and control. Women, who are more likely to adopt collaborative, inclusive, or transformational leadership styles, may face resistance in environments where hierarchical or authoritarian models dominate.

Imposter Syndrome and Confidence:

- Imposter Syndrome is a psychological phenomenon where individuals (particularly women) feel like frauds in their own success, constantly worrying that they don't deserve their position. This stems from societal messages that women aren't naturally suited for leadership, even if they are qualified.

Solutions and Progress:

- Bias training, mentorship, and equal representation in leadership positions are key to reducing bias and increasing the confidence of women in leadership roles. Studies have also shown that when diverse leadership teams are in place, companies often perform better in terms of creativity, decision-making, and overall success.

Section 2: Multitasking vs. Focus

The Myth of Multitasking:

- Multitasking is often glorified in the workplace, especially as a time-saving strategy. However, research suggests that the brain is not actually wired to multitask effectively. In fact, what we call multitasking is often task-switching, which can reduce efficiency, productivity, and quality of work.
    - Example: Answering emails while in a meeting or writing a report while responding to a phone call often results in errors, lack of focus, and mental exhaustion.
- Cognitive Costs of Multitasking: When we switch between tasks, the brain has to recalibrate each time, which leads to mental fatigue and decreases cognitive performance. Studies have shown that multitasking can even reduce memory retention and make it harder to complete complex tasks.

Gendered Expectations Around Multitasking:

- There is an interesting gendered dynamic at play when it comes to multitasking in the workplace. Women are often expected to juggle multiple roles—balancing leadership, emotional labour, and administrative tasks—while men are more likely to be encouraged to focus on singular tasks and specialize in one area.

- Cultural Conditioning: Women are socialized to be more adept at multitasking from an early age (balancing school, home responsibilities, relationships), and this expectation continues into adulthood. In the workplace, this can lead to women taking on extra responsibilities or being expected to manage multiple tasks simultaneously.
- The Productivity Trap: The pressure to multitask may come from an external expectation of efficiency and productivity. While it may seem like multitasking is effective, it's important to note that focused work–spending uninterrupted time on one task–is often more efficient and leads to better results in the long term.

Strategies for Better Focus:

- Time-blocking, setting clear priorities, and eliminating distractions can help individuals improve their focus and productivity. Creating a workplace environment that supports deep work (focused, uninterrupted work) can be a game changer.

Section 3: Emotional Labour in Teams

What is Emotional Labour?

- Emotional labour refers to the process of managing and regulating one's emotions to fulfil the expectations of a job role. It is especially common in services industries or caregiving roles, where employees are required to maintain a positive demean or suppress negative emotions even if they feel otherwise.

- Example: A customer service representative may have to smile, be patient, and provide excellent service even if they are frustrated or upset. Similarly, nurses or teachers often have to maintain a calm, supportive demean or despite their own personal challenges.

Gender and Emotional labour:

- Emotional Labour is particularly gendered, with women often expected to perform more of this invisible work, especially in teams or leadership roles. Women are frequently tasked with emotionally supporting colleagues, providing empathy, and maintaining team morale.
- Example: In many workplaces, women may be more likely to take on the role of mediator or caretaker during conflicts, even if this is not part of their official job description. Men, on the other hand, may be less expected to perform these tasks, which can lead to an unequal distribution of emotional work.

The Costs of Emotional Labour:

- The constant need to manage emotions can lead to burnout, exhaustion, and a phenomenon known as emotional dissonance, where there's a conflict between what an employee feels and what they are expected to display emotionally. This dissonance can have negative consequences for mental health and overall job satisfaction.

- Example: A woman who is constantly expected to display warmth and empathy in her role may begin to feel drained, especially if her own emotional needs are not being met. Over time, this can lead to emotional exhaustion.

Recognizing Emotional Labour in Teams:

- It's important for organizations to acknowledge the role of emotional labour, especially in team dynamics. Emotional labour can lead to unseen contributions that help maintain team cohesion, but it can also create gendered expectations that leave certain individuals, often women, doing more of the emotional work.
- Reducing the Burden: Teams and organizations can mitigate emotional labour by creating a more balanced environment, where emotional support is shared equally and empathy is recognized as a valuable skill, not just a gendered expectation.

Collective Emotional Intelligence:

- Building emotional intelligence (EQ) in teams can help manage emotional labour by ensuring that all members are attuned to each other's emotions and can help distribute emotional support. Leaders who are emotionally intelligent can create a workplace where employees feel safe to express their emotions and support one another.

Chapter 9: Relationships and Love Languages

- How men and women express love
- Conflict resolution styles
- Sex, intimacy, and communication

Section 1: How Men and Women Express Love

Love Languages: The idea of love languages stems from the work of Dr. Gary Chapman, who identified five primary ways people express and receive love:

1. Words of Affirmation
2. Acts of Service
3. Receiving Gifts
4. Quality Time
5. Physical Touch

- Men and Love Languages: Research suggests that men may more commonly express love through physical touch and acts of service, such as fixing things, providing protection, or performing tasks for their partners. This could be tied to biological and social factors, where men have traditionally been socialized to show care through actions rather than verbal expressions.

    - Example: A man might show his love by fixing a broken appliance or taking care of the car, rather than verbally expressing his feelings. This can sometimes be misinterpreted by women, especially if they place more value on verbal affirmations.

- Women and Love Languages: On the other hand, women tend to express love through words of affirmation, quality time, and physical touch. Women are often socialized to be more emotionally expressive, which can make them more comfortable communicating their feelings.
    - Example: A woman may express her love by openly telling her partner she loves him, engaging in deep conversations, or making time for quality activities together like a date night or Cosy evening.

Cultural Influences on Expression:

- Cultural conditioning plays a huge role in shaping how men and women express love. In many cultures, men are expected to hold back emotions and show affection in more subtle ways, while women are encouraged to express their emotions more openly. This can sometimes cause misunderstandings between partners.
- Miscommunication often arises when partners' love languages don't align. For example, a woman who values words of affirmation might feel neglected if her

partner, who expresses love through acts of service, doesn't verbally express his feelings.

Section 2: Conflict Resolution Styles

Gender Differences in Conflict Styles:

- Men and women often approach conflict resolution differently, influenced by both biological factors and socialization.
- Men:
    - Men often have a problem-solving approach to conflict. They may view conflicts as challenges to overcome and often want to resolve the issue quickly. This is part of a broader cultural conditioning where men are taught to be action-oriented and solution-focused.
    - Men may be more likely to withdraw or shut down emotionally when confronted with conflict, sometimes due to a desire to protect their partner or because they don't feel equipped to deal with the emotional aspects of the situation.
    - Example: If a man's partner expresses frustration about something, he might immediately try to fix the issue without fully listening to her emotions, which can come across as dismissive or unempathetic.
- Women:

  - Women, on the other hand, are often taught to prioritize emotional connection and relationship harmony. As a result, women are more likely to engage in emotionally expressive conflict styles, seeking to explore their emotions and the feelings of others involved. They may value the process of conflict resolution as much as the outcome.
  - Women are also more likely to seek resolution through open dialogue and emotional expression, and are generally more comfortable with conflict expression and discussion than men.
  - Example: A woman may want to talk through her feelings during a conflict, seeking reassurance and emotional understanding. If the man isn't receptive or responsive, this can cause frustration, as the emotional connection might not be prioritized.

Conflict Styles and Resolution:

- The key to successful conflict resolution in relationships often lies in finding a balance between these differing styles. Couples who understand that their partner's conflict style is rooted in different needs (emotionally or pragmatically) can more effectively navigate arguments.
- Compromise and Empathy: Learning to listen actively, being empathetic, and allowing space for both emotional expression and problem-solving is

critical. Couples therapy or relationship coaching can also help partners understand how they can bridge the gap in their conflict styles.

Section 3: Sex, Intimacy, and Communication

Sex and Gender Expectations:

- Sexuality and intimacy in relationships are also strongly influenced by gendered expectations. Societal norms often promote certain expectations around how men and women should behave in intimate settings.
- Men:
    - In many societies, men are encouraged to express sexual desire more actively and are often seen as the initiators of sexual encounters. Men's desires and sexual needs are often linked to their physicality, and they are sometimes expected to desire sex frequently.
    - Example: A man may feel pressure to initiate sex in a relationship, even if he's not in the mood, simply because it's seen as his role. If he doesn't initiate, he may feel emasculated or that his manhood is in question.
- Women:
    - On the other hand, women are often socialized to see sex through a lens of emotional connection, where intimacy and

affection are just as important, if not more important, than the physical act itself. Women are often expected to be more emotionally invested in sex.

  - Example: Women may feel pressure to please their partners or to meet certain emotional needs during sex, which can create frustration or performance anxiety if those expectations aren't met.

Gender and Communication Around Sex:

- Communication around sexual intimacy can be challenging in relationships. Men may struggle with expressing vulnerability or discussing sexual needs openly, while women may feel reluctant to communicate their desires out of concern for how they will be perceived or due to concerns about their partner's ego.
- Open dialogue and active communication are essential to ensure both partners' needs are met and that sexual intimacy remains a fulfilling aspect of the relationship.
- Common Issues:
  - Mismatch in Sexual Desire: Differences in libido or sexual preferences can lead to frustration or feelings of rejection if not openly addressed.
  - Performance Anxiety: Both men and women can experience pressure related to sexual

performance, with men often feeling the weight of their role as the initiator or provider of pleasure, and women feeling pressure to be pleasing or "perfect."

Building Intimacy:

- Intimacy isn't just about sex–it's about feeling emotionally connected to your partner. Couples who prioritize emotional intimacy (through vulnerability, shared experiences, and mutual support) tend to have healthier sexual relationships as well.

Practices like non-sexual touch, loving gestures, and deep conversations help build emotional intimacy, which lays a stronger foundation for physical intimacy.

Chapter 10: Finding Common Ground

- Embracing differences without division
- Communication strategies
- How to use knowledge for harmony
- In a world that often highlights our differences—whether biological, emotional, cognitive, or cultural—this chapter focuses on a hopeful truth: understanding our differences can bring us closer together, not push us apart. With the right mindset and tools, we can bridge communication gaps, foster empathy, and build relationships rooted in respect and shared humanity.

Section 1: Embracing Differences Without Division

Difference is Not Deficiency

- Whether it's how men and women express emotion, how trans or nonbinary individuals experience identity, or how neurodivergent minds interpret the world—difference doesn't mean dysfunction. It's simply another way of being.
- Biological and cultural factors influence how we think, feel, and connect—but they should not be used to assign value, rank, or capability.

Why It's Hard to Accept Differences

- Humans are wired for pattern recognition. We instinctively sort people into groups—us vs. them, similar vs. different—as a survival mechanism. But in modern society, this can fuel bias, division, and misunderstanding.
- Our challenge now is to rewire those instincts with awareness and intention, choosing curiosity over judgment.

Shared Goals, Different Paths

- Even when people approach life differently—say, a man may prefer problem-solving while a woman seeks emotional processing—they often want the same thing: connection, respect, understanding. The methods differ, but the destination is shared.

Section 2: Communication Strategies

Understanding is only possible through effective communication. Here are practical, research-backed tools to help people of all identities communicate with clarity, compassion, and openness:

a Active Listening

- Listen not just to respond, but to understand. This means setting aside assumptions and focusing fully on the speaker—tone, body language, and words.
- Reflection technique: Repeat back what the person said in your own words to confirm understanding ("What I'm hearing is...").

b. Language That Connects

- Avoid gendered assumptions. Instead of "You're just being emotional," try "It sounds like this really affected you–can you help me understand?"
- Use inclusive language: "partner" instead of "husband/wife," "they" instead of assuming "he/she."

c. Own Your Perspective

- Use "I" statements to express feelings without blame:
    - "I feel overlooked when my ideas aren't acknowledged."
    - "You never listen to me."

d. Seek Clarification, Not Victory

- Healthy dialogue isn't about winning–it's about learning. Instead of reacting, ask questions:
    - "Can you tell me more about why that matters to you?"
    - "What would make you feel more heard right now?"

e. Make Room for Silence

- Sometimes, quiet is powerful. Let people process. Give space before jumping in. Not everyone communicates at the same speed or in the same way.

Section 3: How to Use Knowledge for Harmony

Understanding brain science, gender theory, and emotional behaviour isn't just academic–it's practical. Here's how to apply the insights from this book to foster connection, respect, and equality:

a. In Relationships

- Recognize that partners may process emotion or solve problems differently–not wrongly.
- Learn each other's love languages, communication styles, and stress responses.
- Choose empathy over efficiency. Sometimes the most helpful response isn't advice–it's simply presence.

b. In the Workplace

- Value both task focus and emotional intelligence.
- Make room for diverse leadership styles, including collaborative and empathetic models.
- Acknowledge and share the burden of emotional labour in teams.

c. In Education and Parenting

- Encourage children to explore identity freely, without being boxed into pink or blue, trucks or dolls.
- Teach emotional literacy to all children, not just girls.
- Foster environments where boys can cry and girls can lead without apology.

d. In Society

- Advocate for inclusive policies and representation across gender and neurodiversity spectrums.
- Challenge stereotypes gently but persistently—whether in media, conversation, or institutions.

Lead by example. Modelling respectful, curiosity-driven dialogue inspires others to do the same

Part IV: Case Studies on Discussion

Chapter 11: Discussion

- Shopping Discussion: Men vs. Women Case studies
- Food Discussion: Men vs. Women
- Discussion on Buying a Car

I'm Different, You're Different - Yet We're Together

Chapter 11: Discussion

- Shopping Discussion: Men vs. Women Case studies
- Food Discussion: Men vs. Women
- Discussion on Buying a Car
- I'm Different, You're Different - Yet We're Together

Section 1: Shopping Discussion: Men vs. Women - 10 Key Differences

Scene: A: Shopping Discussion

Characters:

Jake: The efficiency-loving husband.

Lena: The enthusiastic shopper and "window-shopping

champion." Jake checked his watch.
"Alright. In. Out. One pair of shoes. Max 20 minutes."

Lena raised an eyebrow. "You're adorable."

They stepped into the mall.

Minute 3: Jake found the men's shoe store.
He tried on one pair, walked two steps, and said, "Perfect. I'm done."

Minute 5: He turned around. Lena had vanished.

Minute 8: He found her in a makeup store, holding four lipsticks and debating which shade looked more "sunset-y."

Jake blinked. "Weren't we here for shoes?"

Lena waved him off. "I'm almost done. After this, I want to check out those jeans I saw online. And maybe a new candle."

Minute 18: Jake sat on a bench outside a dressing room, holding four bags.

Minute 36: He started people-watching. Saw two other men also waiting, nodding to them in unspoken solidarity.

Minute 45: Lena emerged triumphantly. "Okay, I just need to check one more place!"

Jake stood up. "Which one?"

She smiled. "You'll see."

Minute 61: Jake had been emotionally broken by scented candles, decorative baskets, and throw pillows. "We don't even have this much couch."

Minute 72: Lena clutched a basket filled with items labelled '*must-haves*' that Jake was sure they'd never use.

He asked, "What about the shoes?"

Lena blinked. "Oh! I totally forgot. Let's go back."

Jake looked to the heavens. "You win

1. Goal vs. Experience

Men: View shopping as a task – go in, buy, get out.

Women: See shopping as an experience – browsing, comparing, and enjoying the process

2. Shopping Time

Men: Prefer quick, focused trips.

Women: Often spend more time exploring options, even without making a purchase.

3. Emotional Motivation

Men: Shop out of necessity (e.g., "I need new shoes").

Women: Shop for mood and emotion (e.g., "This makes me feel confident/happy").

4. Decision-Making Style

Men: Decisive, often choosing the first acceptable item.

Women: Deliberative, compare styles, prices, and reviews before deciding.

5. Use of Technology

Men: Use tech for efficiency (search, buy, done).

Women: Use tech for research (reviews, deals, alternatives) and social sharing.

6. Social Component

Men: Usually prefer shopping alone or with a clear goal.

Women: Often enjoy shopping with others as a bonding activity – even if nothing is bought.

7. Communication While Shopping

Men: Say little; focus on the mission. Less likely to ask for help.

Women: Engage more in conversation, both with companions and store staff. Ask for opinions and give feedback.

8. Reactions to Sales & Discounts

Men: May ignore sales unless it's for a needed item.

Women: More responsive to promotions and deals – may buy just because it's discounted.

9. Variety vs. Utility

Men: Stick to brands or styles they know. Favour utility.

Women: Explore new styles and colours, even buying items they don't "need" but love.

10. Return Behaviour

Men: Less likely to return items – they buy what they trust.

Women: More likely to return or exchange, as they take time to evaluate post-purchase.

Scene: B Saturday Afternoon at the Mall

Jake looked at his watch. *"In and out in 20 minutes,"* he thought. *"She just needs a pair of jeans."*

Lena beamed as they walked in. "Let's stop by Zara first, then H&M. I saw something on Instagram I want to try."

Point 1 – Goal vs. Experience:

Jake's goal is quick shopping. Lena's aim? Explore, enjoy, and discover. Ten minutes in, Lena was already holding three tops and had taken two selfies. She showed Jake a red blouse.
"What do you think of this?"
"It's nice," Jake replied, distracted. "Didn't you say jeans?"

Point 2 – Shopping Time:
Jake's getting impatient; Lena's just warming up.

"Yeah, I need jeans," Lena laughed. "But look at this! It's 40% off. And it matches my boots from last winter."
Jake blinked. "Do you need it?"
"No," she smiled. "But I feel like I've earned it this week."

Point 3 – Emotional Motivation:
For Lena, shopping is also self-care. For Jake, it's about solving a problem.

They eventually found the jeans. Jake picked his pair off the rack, tried it on, and nodded. "Done."
Lena had four options in hand and was texting her sister photos. "Which one looks more flattering?"

Point 4 & 5 – Decision Style & Use of Tech:
Jake made a fast decision. Lena used photos, feedback, and reviews to help decide.

After a while, Jake said, "I'm going to sit near the food court."
Lena smiled. "Okay! I'll meet you in 30. Maybe we can grab coffee after?"

Point 6 – Social Shopping:
For Lena, shopping together = quality time. Jake, however, wants to escape the chaos. On the way out, she grabbed another item. "This bag is on sale. Should I?"
Jake shrugged. "You have like five."
"But this one is different – look at the texture!"
He sighed, silently thinking, *We were supposed to be done.*

Point 7 & 8 – Communication & Discounts:
Lena wants feedback. Jake, unsure how to answer, just wants to leave. She's tempted by the discount – he's not.

Jake had already left with his one purchase in a single bag. Lena had three bags and a receipt for something she might return later.
"I'll see how it looks with my blazer. If not, I'll return it next week," she said.

Point 9 & 10 – Variety & Return Behaviour:
Jake sticks to one brand. Anita enjoys variety – and returns don't bother her.

As they left the mall, Jake smiled and said, "Next time, let's order online."
Lena winked, "Where's the fun in that?"

Moral of the story:
For men, shopping is a *task*.
For women, it's a *tour*.
Men go with a list.
Women leave with a lifestyle.

Section 2. Food Discussion: Men vs. Women

Story: The Dinner Table Debate

It was a chilly Friday evening when six friends gathered around the dining table for a casual dinner party. Among them were Emma and Jake, long-time friends who often found themselves on opposite ends of the food discussion spectrum.

As the dishes arrived–roasted vegetables, a fresh garden salad, grilled steak, and a rich chocolate cake–the conversation naturally drifted toward food.

Emma, serving herself a generous helping of salad, smiled warmly. "I love how colourful and fresh these veggies are.

Eating this way just makes me feel so much healthier and energized."

Jake chuckled, carving into the steak. "I get that, but honestly, nothing beats a good, hearty piece of meat after a long week. It's all about fuelling up and getting that protein boost."

Emma nodded thoughtfully. "I notice I tend to eat slower, savouring each bite. I snack on fruits or nuts throughout the day. What about you?"

Jake shrugged, "I'm usually in and out–fast eater, big portions. Snacking isn't really my thing; I save my appetite for dinner."

As the conversation deepened, Emma shared how she often worries about sugar and tries to avoid processed foods. "I think about what goes into my body a lot. It's probably why I'm always reading labels."

Jake smiled, "I focus more on convenience and taste. I know it's not always the healthiest, but I try to balance with some exercise."

Their friend Mia, listening quietly, added, "I read a study that said men's meat-eating is often linked to cultural ideas of strength and masculinity. That kind of explains Jake's passion for steak!"

Jake laughed, "Maybe so. But honestly, I also appreciate a good burger with the right flavours. It's more about the experience and satisfaction."

Meanwhile, Emma mentioned how she tends to crave sweets more, especially chocolate, and snacks frequently throughout the day. "I think women's brains respond more to food visuals, like desserts and colourful plates. It's emotional, not just hunger."

Jake raised an eyebrow. "That's interesting–I never really thought about food that way. For me, it's mostly about hunger or if something tastes good."

As dessert arrived, the rich chocolate cake sparked a lively debate. Emma expressed guilt over indulging, while Jake shrugged and said, "Life's too short not to enjoy a good dessert now and then!"

The group laughed, realizing how their different perspectives made for a richer, more enjoyable discussion.

By the end of the night, they all agreed: food wasn't just about eating–it was a blend of culture, emotion, health, and identity. Understanding these differences helped them appreciate each other's choices without judgment.

Moral: Food discussions often reveal deeper gendered patterns–like preferences, eating pace, health concerns, and emotional connections. But sharing and respecting these differences can turn any meal into a space for connection and learning.

1. Food Preferences: Meat vs. Fruits & Vegetables

Men typically consume more red and processed meat, whereas women favour fruits, vegetables, yogurt, and whole grains–reflecting differences in dietary taste and cultural norms

2. Taste Preferences: Sweet vs. Salty/Bitter

Women more often prefer sweet or sweet-sour flavours; men gravitate toward salty, umami, or bitter foods and drinks like meat and alcohol.

3. Eating Style: Speed & Portion

Men eat faster, take larger bites, and consume larger portions; women eat more slowly and may graze with smaller portions throughout the day.

4. Health Consciousness

Women tend to show higher health awareness: avoiding sugar, gluten, red meat, and additives more than men—often driven by diet beliefs and health anxiety.

5. Influence of Cultural Masculinity

Men's meat consumption is often tied to ideals of masculinity and strength. Public health researchers note meat-eating as a gender performance rooted in cultural norms.

6. Neural Responses to Food Cues

MRI studies show that women exhibit stronger brain responses to visual cues of food—areas related to reward and emotion—suggesting higher reactivity to food visuals.

7. Cravings & Snacking Habits

Women snack more frequently—often on fruits or sweets—and experience more cravings, while men show greater hunger before dinner and typically snack less.

8. Dieting & Weight Control

Women more commonly practice dietary restraint, dieting, and food tracking due to body image and health beliefs; men more often rely on exercise or ignore dieting unless necessary.

9. Context & Presentation Influence

Studies show that foods presented in a gendered context (e.g"feminine" packaging for salads, "masculine" for burgers) affect taste perception and appeal differently by gender.

10. Social & Conversational Dynamics Around Food

Women more frequently discuss food as part of social bonding, often engaging in "fat talk"—body image-based conversations linked to diet culture. Men usually focus on factual aspects or performance related to eating

Topic	Women	Men
Preferred Foods	Fruits, vegetables, sweet/snack-type foods	Meat, salty/umami foods, hearty meals
Eating Pace & Portion	Slow, smaller bites, frequent snacking	Fast, large bites, less grazing
Health & Diet Awareness	Higher restraint, more health avoidance (e.g., sugar, gluten)	Lower dietary restriction; focus on convenience, protein
Emotional & Social Context	React emotionally, discuss body image, social eating cues	Eat for strength/energy, less social or body-focused dialogue
Response to Food Cues	Greater neural/emotional reactivity to visual food stimuli	Lower reactivity; more utilitarian food view

Section 3: Buying a Car – Different Decision-Making Styles

The Situation:

Emma and her brother Jack are helping their parents choose a new car. They go to a dealership together to look at different options.

- Jack looks at the engine power, speed, and price. He quickly shortlists three cars based on numbers and performance.
- Emma looks at the safety features, comfort, and reviews from families. She wants to talk more about how the car feels to drive and how it will suit the family's needs.

As they discuss:

- Jack says, "This one is fast and fits the budget–why waste time?"
- Emma replies, "But is it safe for long trips with kids? What about the mileage in the city?"

They both get frustrated because they're focused on different things. Their parents appreciate both opinions–but now they're confused too!

How Men Often Think When Buying a Car:

- Interested in engine power, speed, performance
- May care more about brand, styling, or status
- Look at technical specs, modifications, or resale value
- Some enjoy negotiating deals or doing research themselves

Example:
"A man might say, 'I want a car with a turbo engine, good torque, and sporty look.'"

How Women Often Think When Buying a Car:

- Focus on safety features, reliability, and ease of use
- Look for fuel efficiency, comfort, and space (especially if they have a family)
- May care more about colour, feel, tech, or visibility
- Often ask for reviews, trustworthy recommendations, or experience-based advice

Example:
"A woman might say, 'I want a car that's safe for kids, easy to park, and gives good mileage.'"

What We Can Learn:

- Men and women may focus on different things when making choices–some people prefer logic and speed, others think about emotions and safety.
- Both views can be valuable in real-life decisions.
- It's important to listen and balance facts with feelings when making choices together.

1. Key Priorities When Buying a Car (Gender-Wise Breakdown)

Aspect	Men Often Prioritize	Women Often Prioritize
Performance	Engine power, torque, top speed, acceleration	Smoothness, handling, ease of driving

Aspect	Men Often Prioritize	Women Often Prioritize
Design & Looks	Sporty, aggressive, bold	Stylish, practical, clean design
Tech & Features	Infotainment system, engine tuning, driving modes	Navigation, parking assist, connectivity, safety tech
Brand/Status	High-end or performance brands (e.g., BMW, Audi)	Trusted, safe brands (e.g., Toyota, Honda)
Safety	Crash ratings, airbags (less emphasized by some)	Often a top concern—especially for family buyers
Fuel Economy	Important, but may trade for power	Very important; lower running costs matter
Practicality	Secondary priority in some cases	Often primary: boot space, child seat, comfort, parking
Purchase Process	May prefer solo research, faster decisions	Often involve friends/family, ask more questions
Emotional Connection	Status, pride, identity with the car	Trust, comfort, safety vibe with the car

Section 4: I'm Different, You're Different – Yet We're Together

Why She Confused Him

Scene: A Café, Rainy Evening

Characters:

Aarav – A logical, calm-thinking man

Mira – Emotionally expressive and intuitive woman

Aarav (sipping tea):

Mira, I have to ask you something honestly...

Why do you always say something else and mean something else?

Mira (smiling faintly):

I don't. I just expect you to understand without me spelling it all out.

Aarav (confused):

But how? Yesterday you said, "It's fine."

Then didn't talk to me for 2 hours!

Mira: Because "It's fine" means I'm hurt but don't want to argue.

Aarav: See! That's the confusion. Why not just say you're hurt?

Mira: Because I want you to care enough to notice it. Not just respond like a robot.

Aarav (raising eyebrows):

But wouldn't life be easier with direct words?

Mira (softly): Maybe. But emotions are not a math problem.

I feel many things at once – anger, love, fear – and I need to process it.

Aarav (nods slowly): so when I don't react how you expect, you feel I don't care?

Mira: Exactly. It's not confusion... it's layered emotion.

And sometimes, I don't even fully understand what I feel until later.

Aarav: Hmm. So maybe the "confusion" is me not being patient... Not you being unclear.

Mira (smiles): Now you're getting it.

Moral:

Men see clarity as logic.

Women see clarity as being understood without having to explain everything.

The gap isn't confusion – it's a difference in emotional language.

Would you like to add a second part where a woman finds a man confusing too? That would balance the chapter well.

Why He Confused Her

Scene: Same Café, after 15 minutes

Mira (leaning forward): Okay Aarav, now it's my turn.

Sometimes you confuse me too.

Aarav (smiling): Really? I thought I was the clear one.

Mira: That's the thing! You seem clear, but then suddenly pull away emotionally.

Aarav: I'm not pulling away. I just need space to think.

Mira: See? That "space" feels like rejection to me.

You go quiet, stop texting, and I start imagining the worst.

Aarav: But when I'm stressed or unsure, I go into "solve-it-alone" mode. It's how I was raised – don't show weakness.

Mira (softly): But when you shut down, I feel like you don't trust me with your emotions.

Aarav: It's not about trust. It's about not knowing how to talk about it.

Mira: Then tell me that at least – say "I need some time."

Don't just disappear into silence.

Aarav: You're right. I guess my silence speaks a language you don't understand.

Mira: And your logic sometimes feels... too cold.

Like when I share how I feel, and you try to "fix" it instead of just listening.

Aarav (laughs): That's the engineer in me. I want solutions.

Mira: Sometimes, I don't want solutions. I want connection.

Moral:

Women confuse men with emotions.

Men confuse women with silence and logic.

Understanding grows when both stop reacting – and start listening.

Part V: How men and women Think

Chapter 12: Way of thinking

- The Silent Treatment vs The Need to Talk
- Jealousy and Insecurity: Gendered Reactions
- Ego vs Emotion: What Hurts Whom More
- Who Apologizes First – and why?
- Love Languages: How Each Gender Shows and Feels Love
- Thinking During a Fight: Instant vs Delayed Processors
- Financial Thinking: Risk vs Stability
- Fear of Losing Respect vs Fear of Losing Love
- Dreams and Ambition: Whose Career Wins in a Relationship
- Avoid Arguments
- Einstein's Silent Brain

Chapter 12: Way of thinking

- The Silent Treatment vs The Need to Talk
- Jealousy and Insecurity: Gendered Reactions
- Ego vs Emotion: What Hurts Whom More
- Who Apologizes First – and why?
- Love Languages: How Each Gender Shows and Feels Love
- Thinking During a Fight: Instant vs Delayed Processors
- Financial Thinking: Risk vs Stability
- Fear of Losing Respect vs Fear of Losing Love
- Dreams and Ambition: Whose Career Wins in a Relationship
- Avoid Arguments

Section 1. The Silent Treatment vs The Need to Talk

A Why men often go silent under stress.

Stress doesn't just challenge the body it challenges the mind. And when it hits, men and women often take very different cognitive and emotional paths. One of the most noticeable behaviours? Men go quiet. Not because they don't care – but because silence, for many men, is survival.

1. The Male Brain Under Pressure

When a man is under stress, his brain prioritizes problem-solving over verbal processing. The amygdala (the brain's alarm system) activates, and blood flow is often redirected away from the prefrontal cortex, where reasoning and speech occur. Instead of talking through a problem, many men instinctively go internal thinking through it silently.

2. Silence as a Coping Mechanism

For many men, silence is not avoidance it's containment. It's a way to:

- Avoid saying something in anger,
- Regain control of their emotions, and
- Solve the problem mentally before speaking out loud.
- This often contrasts with women, who are more inclined to process stress externally by talking through emotions in real time.

3. Conditioned to Withhold Emotion

From a young age, boys are taught messages like:

Don't cry, Be a man, Deal with it.

Over time, this leads many men to believe that expressing stress verbally is weakness, and silence is strength. In adulthood, this belief becomes a reflex. When stressed, they withdraw, not because they don't feel – but because they were never taught how to express it safely.

4. The Fear of Emotional Escalation

Another reason men go quiet? They fear that talking while emotionally charged will escalate the situation or expose their vulnerability.
So silence becomes a shield:

"If I speak now, I might say the wrong thing. " Better to stay silent than lose control. "To partners, this may feel like emotional abandonment. To the man, it feels like restraint.

5. The Thinking Difference: Internal vs External Processors
Stress highlights a key difference:

- Men are often internal processors - they think first, speak later (if at all).
- Women tend to be external processors - they speak to clarify what they feel.

This mismatch creates tension in relationships:

- She needs connection to feel safe.
- He needs silence to feel in control.

Without understanding this difference, both feel misunderstood.

6. Bridging the Silence Gap

The solution isn't to force men to talk more, or women to talk less – it's to build mutual understanding:

- Men can learn that sharing stress doesn't make them weak.
- Women can learn that his silence is often effort, not indifference.

A healthy compromise might be:

"I need 30 minutes to process this – but I promise we'll talk after."

B Why women want to discuss problems immediately.

When conflict arises, many women feel an urgent need to talk it out – now. To a male partner, this can seem overwhelming or "too much." To her, waiting feels unbearable. Why? Because for many women, communication isn't optional – it's regulation.

1. The Female Brain and Connection Under Stress

When a woman is stressed, her brain typically releases higher levels of oxytocin – a hormone linked to bonding, comfort, and social connection. This makes women more likely to seek closeness, especially through verbal expression.

Talking doesn't just process the problem – it soothes the nervous system.

2. Emotion Needs to Move

For women, emotion is not something to be "solved" – it's something to be felt and expressed.
Verbalizing what's wrong helps:

- Reduce internal pressure
- Gain clarity through dialogue
- Feel seen and understood

Holding it in often feels like emotional suffocation. That's why waiting to talk feels worse than the issue itself.

3. Social Conditioning: Keep the Peace, Maintain Connection

From a young age, girls are taught to value emotional harmony:

- "Talk about your feelings."

- "Say sorry."
- "Don't let things fester."

As adults, this becomes urgency: when something is off, it must be addressed immediately or the relationship feels unsafe.

4. Silence Feels Like Rejection

When a man withdraws or goes quiet, a woman may interpret it as:

- Emotional abandonment
- Passive aggression
- A sign that the relationship is breaking

Because women often associate closeness with communication, silence during conflict feels like disconnection. And disconnection feels threatening.

5. External Processors Need Dialogue to Think

Many women are external processors – they figure out what they feel by talking it out.

- It's not always about having a solution.
- It's about making sense of the emotion.

When asked to "just think about it quietly," many women feel lost, anxious, or disconnected from themselves and their partner.

6. The Urgency Is Emotional, Not Logical
7. To many men, this urgency can feel excessive – "Why does it have to be now?"

But for women, the need to talk isn't about control – it's about safety.

8. If we talk, we're connected.
   If we delay, we're drifting.
9. The faster the repair, the less internal damage.

Real conversation examples + solutions.

Scene: "We Need to Talk" vs. "Not Now"

Her: "Can we please talk about what happened earlier? I hate going to bed like this."

Him: "Seriously? Right now? I'm exhausted. Can't we just drop it?"

Her (hurt): "Of course you want to drop it. You never care about how I feel."

Him (defensive): "That's not true. I just don't want to fight."

What's Really Happening?

- She feels anxious and unsettled. The problem is still "open," and her emotional system needs connection and clarity to feel safe.
- He feels drained and overwhelmed. He needs space to process privately and avoid a heated conflict.

Solution: Time-Bound Reassurance

Her: "I'm not trying to fight. I just need to know we're okay before I can sleep."

Him: "I hear you. I'm not in the right headspace to talk now, but I promise I'll be clear and present tomorrow morning. Can we do that?"

Her: "Okay. I just needed to know we're not sweeping it under the rug."

Tip for Men:

Reassurance is powerful. Saying *"I'm not avoiding you, I just need space"* helps her feel secure even in silence.

Tip for Women:

Delaying doesn't mean he's withdrawing love – it might mean he's trying not to *explode or shut down*. Letting him breathe can bring better results.

Section 2. Jealousy and Insecurity: Gendered Reactions

A How women react when they feel emotionally threatened.

When women feel emotionally threatened–whether in romantic relationships, friendships, or family dynamics–their reactions can vary widely depending on personality, context, and past experiences. However, some common emotional and behavioural patterns do emerge, often shaped by gender socialization and emotional coping styles. Here's a focused overview of how many women tend to react when they feel emotionally threatened:

1. Heightened Emotional Sensitivity

Women may become more sensitive to perceived slights, rejections, or changes in emotional tone.

- Reading between the lines of what's said–or left unsaid.

- Noticing subtle shifts in attention, affection, or behaviour.
- Becoming more reactive to minor conflicts or perceived distance.

2. Increased Need for Reassurance

An emotional threat often triggers insecurity, leading to a desire for confirmation that the relationship or connection is still safe.

- Asking questions like: *"Do you still care about me?"* or *"Are you mad at me?"*
- Seeking more frequent texts, calls, or physical closeness.
- Wanting verbal affirmations of love, loyalty, or attention.

3. Withdrawal or Silent Treatment

If direct confrontation feels risky or uncomfortable, some women may emotionally shut down instead.

- Becoming quiet, distant, or emotionally unavailable.
- Saying "I'm fine" when they aren't, hoping the other person will notice and respond.
- Using silence as a protective wall rather than a punishment.

4. Overthinking and Rumination

Many women process emotional pain by mentally replaying events, analysing conversations, or imagining worst-case scenarios.

- Replaying an argument or comment repeatedly in their mind.
- Trying to "figure out" what changed or went wrong.
- Doubting themselves or their worth.

5. Jealousy and Comparison

An emotional threat can trigger jealousy, especially if another person seems to be "replacing" them.

- Comparing themselves to others in terms of looks, attention, status, or connection.
- Feeling jealous of a partner's time or energy spent elsewhere.
- Worrying they're not "enough" in some way.

6. Indirect Communication

Rather than openly expressing pain or fear, emotional distress might come out in more subtle or coded ways.

- Passive-aggressive comments or behaviour.
- Hinting instead of stating what they feel directly.
- Testing the other person's love or loyalty without explicitly saying why.

7. Heightened Attachment or Clinginess (in anxious styles)

Some women, especially those with anxious attachment styles, may respond by trying to close the gap emotionally.

- Becoming more "clingy" or dependent on the person who triggered the threat.
- Fearing abandonment or rejection.

- Trying harder to please or prove their worth.

8. Defensive or Reactive Behaviour

If the emotional threat is intense or ongoing, some women may become more assertive or confrontational.

- Accusing their partner of being distant, dishonest, or disloyal.
- Setting emotional boundaries or issuing ultimatums.
- Expressing anger or frustration more openly.

9. Seeking External Support

Talking to trusted friends or confidants is a common coping mechanism.

- Venting to someone safe for emotional clarity or comfort.
- Getting validation or a second opinion on what's going on.
- Sometimes using social media or public signals to express discontent indirectly.

B How men react when they feel disrespected or replaced.

When men feel disrespected or replaced—especially in close relationships or status-driven environments—their reactions often differ from women's due to a combination of biology, social conditioning, and individual personality. These feelings can threaten a man's sense of identity, masculinity, or emotional security, leading to a range of emotional and behavioural responses.

Here's a clear breakdown of how many men tend to react in these situations:

When Men Feel Disrespected

1. Anger or Defensiveness

- Quick escalation: Disrespect often triggers anger first, as it hits pride or perceived status.
- Verbal confrontation: Responding with sarcasm, argument, or raised tone.
- Defensive posture: Justifying themselves or shifting blame to regain control.

2. Withdrawal or Stonewalling

- Shutting down emotionally.
- Going quiet, walking away from conflict, or refusing to engage.
- A way to avoid vulnerability or perceived weakness.

3. Overcompensation

- Acting more dominant, assertive, or even aggressive.
- Showing off, making power plays, or asserting control in other areas (e.g., work, gym, social media).
- Trying to regain a sense of value or control.

4. Loss of Respect for the Other Person

- Pulling back emotionally from someone they feel disrespected by.
- Seeing them as less trustworthy or less important.

- Sometimes leading to emotional detachment or even infidelity.

5. Attempts to Reclaim Respect

- Setting firm boundaries ("You won't talk to me like that").
- Seeking validation from others (especially male peers).
- Trying to reassert leadership or influence in the relationship.

Section 3. Ego vs Emotion: What Hurts Whom More?

A discussion about how women hurt emotionally, and men hurt silently through ego wounds.

How women and men often experience emotional pain differently, especially in intimate relationships. It reflects both psychological tendencies and cultural conditioning, not just biology. Let's break this down into a meaningful, respectful discussion:

How Women Tend to Hurt Emotionally

1. Emotionally Open Pain

Women are often socialized to express vulnerability and seek emotional connection when hurt.

- They cry, talk, or reach out to others.
- Emotional pain is often verbalized: *"That hurt me,"* or *"I feel unimportant."*

- There's a desire for understanding, validation, and repair through dialogue.

2. Relational Wounding

- Many women experience emotional pain when they feel emotionally disconnected, rejected, or unseen.
- Emotional neglect or lack of atonement can feel like abandonment.
- They often ask: *"Am I not enough?", "Why don't you open up to me?"*

3. Self-Blame & Overthinking

- Pain often gets internalized–they question their value, attractiveness, or worth.
- They may replay events, trying to figure out what went wrong and how to fix it.

How Men Tend to Hurt Silently Through Ego Wounds

1. Ego = Identity

For many men, the ego isn't just pride–it's tied to how they see themselves: capable, respected, protective, wanted.

- When a man feels rejected, criticized, or not needed, it strikes at his core identity, not just his emotions.

2. Pain Hidden as Silence or Anger

- Instead of saying *"That hurt me,"* many men go quiet, shut down, or get angry.
- They've often been taught that showing vulnerability is weak or unmanly.

- So they bottle pain, and it leaks out through distance, defensiveness, or detachment.

A man rarely says "My feelings are hurt." He might say "Whatever, do what you want," while silently feeling replaced or disrespected.

3. Rejection = Ego Collapse

- If a partner chooses someone else, mocks his effort, or disrespects his contribution, it can feel like a personal failure.
- Even small slights (mocking his job, criticizing his efforts, not appreciating what he provides) can cut deeply.
- Instead of expressing pain, he may try to reclaim his ego—through control, withdrawal, or sometimes infidelity.

Why the Difference?

Social Conditioning:

- Women are often encouraged to name and process feelings, build emotional language, and seek connection.
- Men are often taught to solve problems, tough it out, and not show pain—especially emotional pain.

Psychological Tendencies:

- Women tend to connect pain with relational disconnection.

- Men tend to connect pain with loss of respect, control, or worth.

How to Bridge the Gap

When Women Hurt	When Men Hurt	How to Heal
Need to be heard, understood, emotionally held	Need to feel respected, trusted, not emasculated	Use both softness and clarity. Validate emotions without blame.
May over-communicates, become emotionally intense	May shut down or become sarcastic or cold	Avoid shaming or pushing. Invite honesty by being emotionally safe.
Feel pain from emotional distance	Feel pain from perceived inadequacy or loss of value	Ask: "*What are you feeling, not just thinking?*" Encourage healthy expression.

Final Thought

Men and women both hurt deeply, but the pain often wears different faces.

- Women bleed emotionally–seeking closeness to soothe pain.
- Men bleed internally–through ego wounds that silence and isolate them.

Understanding this difference can transform how partners relate, love, and support each other–because beneath it all, both just want to feel safe, valued, and loved.

Example

fictional dialogue that shows how a woman expresses emotional pain openly, while a man experiences it silently through an ego wound. This example highlights how they misunderstand each other at first, but begin to reconnect when both become emotionally honest.

Scene: A Couple After an Argument

Characters: Layla and Marcus, in a long-term relationship. Layla feels emotionally neglected. Marcus feels criticized and unappreciated.

Initial Conflict (Miscommunication & Misunderstanding)

Layla *(frustrated)*: "I feel like I'm invisible to you lately. I try to talk, but you barely respond. It's like I don't matter anymore."

Marcus *(coldly)*: "Here we go again. I work all day, and somehow that means I don't care about you?"

Layla: "I'm not saying you don't care. I'm saying I *don't feel* close to you. You never open up. I'm always the one reaching."

Marcus *(defensive)*: "Maybe I don't open up because every time I do, it's not enough. There's always something I'm doing wrong."

What's Happening:
Layla is speaking directly from emotional pain—she feels disconnected.
Marcus hears criticism, and his ego is wounded. He feels unappreciated and shuts down.

Emotional Block (Pain Behind Ego)

Layla *(softer)*: "I'm not trying to attack you, Marcus. I miss you. I miss *us*. I feel like I'm reaching and you're pulling away."

Marcus *(quiet)*: "I don't know what to say. It's like no matter what I do, I'm just... not enough."

Layla *(pauses)*: "...Is that how it feels?"

Marcus: "Yeah. When you say I don't open up, I hear 'you're a bad partner.' I don't know how to fix that. I feel like I'm failing you."

What's Happening:
Marcus finally admits the real issue: he feels inadequate, not indifferent. His ego pain was masking emotional hurt.

Reconnection (Emotional Truth + Respect)

Layla *(gently)*: "I never meant to make you feel like you're failing. I just need to feel close to you again. I don't need perfect. I need *real*."

Marcus: "I want that too. But I don't always know how to say what I'm feeling. I'm not good at it."

Layla: "You don't have to be perfect with your words. Just be here. Just try."

Marcus *(nods)*: "I can do that. I want to."

What's Happening:
They move past ego and defines into mutual understanding. Layla softens her approach; Marcus lowers his guard.

Lesson

- Layla's pain was emotional absence: feeling unseen, emotionally disconnected.
- Marcus's pain was ego-based: feeling like a failure, emotionally inadequate.

- When both expressed the truth beneath the reaction, they were able to reconnect.

Example: A woman says "You never understand me" vs a man hears "You're a failure."

Emma *(upset)*: “You never understand me. I tell you how I feel, and it’s like I’m talking to a wall.”

William *(tense)*: “I’m trying. I do everything for this relationship and it’s still not enough?”

Emma *(raising voice)*: “It’s not about what you *do*! It’s that I don’t feel emotionally seen.”

William *(shuts down)*: “Alright. I’m clearly just a disappointment then. Thanks.”

What’s *Actually* Happening Emotionally

- Emma is saying: “I feel emotionally disconnected and alone. I need empathy and emotional presence.”
- William *hears*: “You’re failing as a man and a partner. You’re not good enough.”

This disconnect happens because:

- She communicates pain through emotional language.
- He receives it as a judgment of competence or identity–a direct hit to the ego.

Rebuilding the Bridge (Emotionally Attuned Conversation)

Emma *(calmer)*: “When I said you don’t understand me, I wasn’t saying you’re a failure. I was saying I feel alone in how I experience things.”

William (pauses): "I heard it like I wasn't enough. Like I'm not what you need."

Emma "I don't need you to be perfect. I need to feel like you're *with me* when I'm struggling. That's it."

William (softer): "Okay. That helps. I can try to be more present... even if I don't always know what to say. " Insight

Woman Says	Man Often Hears	Underlying Message
"You never understand me."	"You're failing as a partner."	"I feel emotionally alone and need empathy, not solutions."
"You don't listen."	"You're not good enough."	"I want you to be emotionally available, not distracted."
"You've changed."	"I'm not desirable anymore."	"I miss how close we used to be."

Takeaway

Women often express emotional needs as frustrations.
Men often interpret those frustrations as failures.

Both are hurting. One is asking to be heard.
The other is trying not to feel useless.

The bridge is built when both realize: *"We're not against each other. We're both trying to feel safe and loved."*

Section 4: Apologizes

1 Who Apologizes First – and why?

"Who apologizes first?" is often less about gender and more about emotional wiring, communication style, and attachment patterns. But when looking at common dynamics between men and women, there are trends in how and why each tends to apologize (or avoid it), shaped by culture and emotion.

Who Tends to Apologize First – Men or Women?

In general: Women tend to apologize first more often than men – but not necessarily because they're more at fault. The reasons are largely psychological, social, and emotional.

Why Women Tend to Apologize First

1. Social Conditioning
    - From a young age, many women are taught to be caretakers of emotional harmony.
    - Saying "I'm sorry" becomes a reflex to soothe conflict or rebuild connection.
2. Sensitivity to Relationship Tension
    - Women often have a lower tolerance for emotional disconnection in close relationships.
    - They may apologize simply to get the emotional bond back on track – even if they're still hurt.
3. Stronger Emotional Vocabulary
    - Many women are more practiced in recognizing and naming emotions, which helps them take responsibility more quickly.

Women Often Apologize First Why?

- Women are usually socialized to preserve harmony in relationships.
- Many feel more comfortable naming emotions and taking responsibility for hurt – even if they didn't cause it.
- They may apologize to de-escalate a conflict and reconnect, not necessarily because they're wrong.

Example: "I'm sorry things got tense earlier. I hate when we fight. I just wanted to feel understood." Even if she's hurt, she may lead with softness to open the emotional door again.

Why Men Often Apologize Later (or Less Often)

1. Ego & Identity Tied to Being "Right" or Strong
   - Apologizing can feel like admitting failure or showing vulnerability, which many men have been taught to avoid.
2. Fear of Losing Respect
   - For some men, apologizing feels like losing status or control, especially if they already feel disrespected.
3. Different Conflict Thresholds
   - Men may not recognize emotional harm as quickly – especially if it's subtle or unspoken.
   - A man might think: "*Why should I apologize? We just had a disagreement.*"

Men Often Wait Longer to Apologize (If at All) Why?

- Men are often taught to value pride, control, and emotional stoicism.
- Apologizing can feel like admitting failure or weakness, especially if their ego is already bruised.
- If the argument made them feel disrespected **or** emasculated, they may shut down rather than open up.

Example**:** "Yeah, I lost my temper. I guess I could've handled it better."

Less direct. More guarded. It's often their version of an apology.

Emotional Drivers Behind Apologizing

Studies Support This

Research shows:

- Women apologize more often – not because they do more wrong, but because they're more likely to see something as apology-worthy.
- Men tend to underestimate the emotional impact of their words/actions, so they may not see a need to apologize at all.

Women	Men
Seek connection and repair	Seek respect and stability
View apology as an emotional bridge	View apology as loss of status

Women	Men
Apologize even when not fully at fault	Often apologize only when clearly at fault
Fear of being emotionally rejected	Fear of being seen as weak or inferior

What Matters More Than Who Apologizes First?

- **Emotional maturity:** The ability to apologize without defensiveness.
- **Security:** Feeling safe enough to be vulnerable.
- **Timing:** An apology offered too soon (to avoid discomfort) or too late (after damage builds) may both miss the mark.

In a Healthy Relationship

Sometimes she apologizes first because she feels everything too deeply.
Sometimes he waits because he feels too much but hasn't learned how to say it. The healthiest dynamic is when both people can say:

"I care more about us than about being right. I'm sorry for my part in the hurt."

Gender differences in ego, guilt, and the willingness to say sorry. Cultural programming behind it.

Section 5: Love Languages: How Each Gender Shows and Feels Love

A Touch, time, gifts, words, help – which one's men prefer vs women?

1. Physical Touch

Description:

- Includes hugging, holding hands, kissing, cuddling, sex, or just being physically close.
- It's not always sexual – it's about connection through contact.

Men Often Prefer Touch:

- Physical touch is frequently a man's primary love language.
- It affirms desirability, affection, and emotional closeness.
- Many men feel most loved when they are wanted physically.

Women's View of Touch:

- Often need emotional safety first before fully opening to physical affection.
- Touch is welcome when it's connected to emotional intimacy, not just physical desire.

2. Quality Time

Description:

- Focused, undistracted time together. Deep conversation, shared activities, or simple presence.

Women Often Prefer Time:

- Crave emotional presence and intentional moments together.

- Listening, eye contact, and shared attention are signs of love and emotional security.

Men's View of Time:

- May enjoy quality time, but less likely to equate it directly with love.
- Some men prefer parallel activities (watching TV, doing something together), rather than direct emotional engagement.

3. Gifts

Description:

- Physical symbols of thoughtfulness. Doesn't have to be expensive – it's about meaning, not money.

Women Appreciate Sentimental Gifts:

- Many associate gifts with being remembered, cherished, or seen.
- The emotional thought behind the gift matters more than the item itself.

Men View Gifts Differently:

- Fewer men list this as a primary love language.
- If they value gifts, it's usually in practicality or symbolism, not emotion.
- May feel awkward receiving gifts unless tied to achievement or tradition.

4. Words of Affirmation

Description:

- Verbal expressions of love, appreciation, encouragement, and validation.

Women Strongly Respond to Words:

- Words make emotions visible. "I love you," "You matter," or "I see you" can go a long way.
- Many women feel emotionally disconnected without verbal affirmation.

Men Also Crave Words – Quietly:

- Men may not say they need it, but often long to hear appreciation and respect.
- Praise like "I'm proud of you" or "You handled that well" builds self-worth and connection.

5. Help (Acts of Service)

Description:

- Doing helpful things to ease the other person's burden: chores, errands, fixing something, making food.

Women Often Feel Loved Through Service:

- Small efforts (like making tea, taking care of the kids, cleaning up) = *"I see you, I care."*
- These acts represent reliability, support, and attentiveness.

Men Express Love Through Service:

- Men may not say "I love you" often, but they'll build the shelves, fix the car, or pay the bills to show it.

- Acts of service are often how men show love, even if it's not how they receive it.

Final Summary Table

Love Language	Women Tend To Prefer	Men Tend To Prefer
Touch	When emotionally safe	As affirmation and desire
Quality Time	For emotional bonding	For shared activity
Words	For reassurance and closeness	For validation and respect
Gifts	When symbolic and personal	Less frequent, practical
Acts of Service	As proof of care	As way of showing love

B How mismatched love languages create distance.

Mismatched love languages are one of the most common but silent reasons couples feel unloved, even when both are trying hard. Let's break down how love language mismatches create emotional distance – with examples and solutions.

What Is a Mismatched Love Language?

A mismatch happens when one person gives love in the way *they* prefer, but their partner feels loved in a completely different way.

Example:

- Partner A feels loved through words.

- Partner B shows love through acts of service.

Result:
Partner B might be fixing the car, cleaning the house – while Partner A feels emotionally neglected because they never hear *"I love you."*

How Mismatches Create Distance (Topic-Wise)

1. Physical Touch vs. Acts of Service

- One partner needs touch to feel loved.
- The other shows love by doing tasks, not touching.

Result:
The touch-oriented partner feels rejected and unwanted, even though the other person feels they're being loving and helpful.

Common feeling:

"They never reach for me. I feel like we're roommates."

2. Quality Time vs. Words of Affirmation

- One person wants deep, undivided time together.
- The other sends sweet texts and compliments, thinking that's enough.

Result:
The time-oriented partner feels emotionally disconnected. The words fall flat without presence.

Common feeling:

"They're sweet, but never really *with* me."

3. Words vs. Touch

- One needs verbal reassurance: "You're amazing. I love you."
- The other expresses love by physical intimacy, not talking much.

Result:
The verbal partner feels insecure, like the other is emotionally distant.
The touch-oriented one feels confused: *"I hug you every day – how can you not feel loved?"*

Common feeling:

"They're affectionate but never say anything meaningful."

4. Gifts vs. Acts of Service

- One person gives thoughtful gifts to say "I love you."
- The other wants help, not things – or vice versa.

Result:
Gifts feel shallow. Acts feel invisible.

Common feeling:

"They keep buying me things I don't need – but won't help when I'm overwhelmed."

What Is a Love Language Mismatch?

A mismatch happens when two people express and receive love in different ways – so even with good intentions, the love isn't felt.

It's like pouring effort into a relationship but in the wrong emotional currency.

Topic-Wise Breakdown of Common Mismatches

1. Words of Affirmation vs. Acts of Service

- Person A needs: Encouraging words, compliments, verbal affection
- Person B gives: Help – cleaning, fixing, organizing

Problem:
Person A feels unloved because they never hear *"I love you"* or *"I'm proud of you"*, even though Person B is constantly doing things behind the scenes.

Emotional Impact:

- A feels unappreciated.
- B feels unrecognized for their efforts.
- *Both are loving. Neither feels loved.*

2. Physical Touch vs. Quality Time

- Person A needs: Hugging, holding hands, physical closeness
- Person B gives: Time – going out together, having deep talks

Problem:
One feels emotionally starved without touch. The other feels they're doing their best by showing up and being present.

Emotional Impact:

- A feel unwanted or sexually rejected.
- B feels confused: *"We spent all day together. What's missing?"*

Closeness becomes frustrating instead of connecting.

3. Gifts vs. Acts of Service

- Person A needs: Thoughtful, symbolic gifts – something that says *"I remembered you"*
- Person B gives: Practical help – doing the laundry, making meals

Problem:
Gifts feel shallow to B. Acts feel unnoticed by A.

Emotional Impact:

- A feels uncherished – *"You never surprise me with anything."*
- B feels misunderstood – *"I'm doing everything to make your life easier!"*

Effort doesn't translate into emotional fulfilment.

4. Quality Time vs. Words of Affirmation

- Person A needs: Presence and undivided attention
- Person B gives: Constant compliments and verbal check-ins

Problem:
A wants depth and shared space. B thinks texting "I love you" daily is enough.

Emotional Impact:

- A feels emotionally distant.
- B feels they're doing more than enough.

Words feel hollow without presence. Presence feels unseen without verbal warmth.

How to Repair a Mismatch

1. Learn Each Other's Love Language

- Use a love language quiz or simply ask:
- "What makes you feel most loved – what I say, do, give, or how I spend time with you?"

2. Switch from Giving to Translating

- Don't just give love – translate it into your partner's language.
- Example: Instead of saying *"I love you"*, show it by being physically close – *if that's what they need.*

3. Communicate Needs Without Blame

- Instead of:
- "You never make me feel loved."
  Say:
  "I feel most connected when we cuddle / when you say something kind / when we spend time just us."

Section 6. Thinking During a Fight: Instant vs Delayed Processors

A Women often want to resolve conflict immediately.

Why Women Want Immediate Resolution?

1. Emotional Tension Feels Unsafe

- Unresolved conflict often feels like emotional abandonment or disconnection.
- The longer the silence, the stronger the anxiety.

"If we don't talk now, will we drift further apart?"

2. Relational Thinking

- Women are often more attuned to emotional dynamics and interpersonal harmony.
- They often feel responsible for keeping the emotional bond intact.

"I can't relax if we're not okay."

3. Verbal Processing

- Many women process emotion out loud – they need to talk it through to understand how they feel.
- Silence feels like punishment, not reflection.

"If we don't talk, nothing will get fixed."

4. Fear of Emotional Shutdown

- Delayed responses may feel like the partner is withdrawing emotionally – which can trigger deeper fears of rejection.

"If he really cared, he'd stay and talk."

When a woman pushes for immediate resolution, it's often not about "being dramatic" or "controlling the moment." It's usually this:

"I feel unsafe when we're not emotionally connected. Let's fix it before the distance becomes damage."

But if her partner isn't ready to talk, this urgency may backfire – making him shut down more, which increases her anxiety... and a loop begins.

Healthier Approach for Instant Processors (Often Women)

1. Recognize urgency isn't always effective
   - Pressing harder can feel like an attack to someone who needs space.
2. Pause – with a plan
   - Say: "I want to talk and reconnect. When you're ready, can we do that soon?"
3. Regulate emotions before pushing for answers
   - Ask: "Am I trying to fix it... or escape the discomfort of uncertainty?"

When Instant and Delayed Processors Clash

Instant Processor (Often Woman)	**Delayed Processor (Often Man)**
Feels unloved by silence	Feels trapped by urgency
Wants verbal resolution now	Needs internal clarity first
Thinks silence = punishment	Thinks space = safety

B Men may take time to process emotions and thoughts.

Many men need time to process their emotions and thoughts during or after conflict. This isn't avoidance or indifference – it's often how they cope with stress, regulate emotions, and think clearly.

Let's explore why men tend to be delayed emotional processors, how it plays out in relationships, and what can help both partners navigate it better.

Why Many Men Take Time to Process Emotions

1. Internal Processing Style

- Many men process internally, not verbally.
- They often need quiet or solitude to figure out *what they feel*, *why they feel it*, and *what to say about it*.

"Let me sit with this before I respond."

2. Avoiding Escalation

- When emotions run high, men may fear saying something harmful or losing control.
- They withdraw to avoid making things worse.

"If I talk now, I'll just make it worse."

3. Cultural Conditioning

- Many men were taught to suppress emotions rather than name them.
- So when emotions rise, the response is often to shut down, not express.

"I don't even know what I'm feeling yet – how can I explain it?"

4. Ego & Identity Protection

- Conflict can feel like a direct hit to their competence or value.

- Men may pull back until they can restore a sense of self-worth or stability.

"I need to cool off before I feel like myself again."

Common Conflict Pattern

She (Instant Processor)	He (Delayed Processor)
Wants to talk now	Needs space to think
Presses for answers	Withdraws to calm down
Feels abandoned	Feels overwhelmed

Section 7: Financial Thinking: Risk vs Stability

- A Why men may focus on investment, risk, and growth.
- The tendency for men to focus more on investment, risk, and growth—especially in financial or business contexts—can be understood through a combination of evolutionary psychology, social conditioning, economic structures, and individual personality traits. Here's a breakdown:

1. Evolutionary Psychology

- Historically, males competed for resources and mates, which may have encouraged risk-taking behaviours.
- Risk and reward strategies often conferred status, which in evolutionary terms could increase social power or reproductive success.

- Traits like dominance, competitiveness, and ambition–which align with investment and growth thinking–were often selected for.

2. Cultural and Social Conditioning

- Boys are often encouraged to compete, take initiative, and build wealth or success as a measure of self-worth.
- Traditional masculinity often values:
    - Independence → "Make your own way."
    - Provision → "Be the breadwinner."
    - Control → "Don't rely on anyone else."

This cultural messaging pushes many men toward:

High-growth ventures, aggressive investing, and risk-taking as identity markers.

3. Economic Roles and Expectations

- In many societies, men have historically been primary earners, incentivizing long-term investment thinking and aggressive financial strategies.
- Business and finance sectors, which emphasize growth and leverage, have been male-dominated, reinforcing a risk-oriented environment.

4. Biological Factors

- Testosterone has been loosely linked to increased risk appetite and reward-seeking behaviour.
- Neurological studies show that men may respond more strongly to potential upside in competitive

scenarios (e.g., financial games or stock trading simulations).

5. Psychological and Cognitive Differences

- Men are statistically more likely to:
    - Be overconfident in financial decision-making.
    - Trade more frequently (and sometimes less successfully).
    - Be comfortable with volatility and uncertainty.

6. Identity and Legacy Thinking

- Many men tie their sense of purpose or self-worth to what they build or grow—whether a business, a portfolio, or a legacy.
- Long-term investment and risk-taking can be viewed as ways to leave a mark, gain freedom, or achieve status.

B Why women often prioritize security, stability, and budgeting.

The tendency for many women to prioritize security, stability, and budgeting—especially in financial decision-making—has deep roots in evolution, culture, and lived experience. This doesn't mean women avoid risk entirely, but they often approach it more cautiously and strategically. Here's a breakdown of the main reasons:

1. Evolutionary Psychology

- In ancestral environments, resource stability was critical for child-rearing and survival.
- Women often took on roles that required long-term planning, risk avoidance, and resource conservation—traits passed down through generations.
- Emotional and physical security for the family was vital, so cautious decision-making had evolutionary advantages.

2. Social Conditioning & Gender Roles

- Girls are often raised to:
    - Be careful, nurturing, and prudent.
    - Avoid mistakes or dangers ("Don't take chances").
    - Take responsibility for household management and family well-being.

This leads to a mindset focused on: *"Make sure everything is covered, protected, and planned for."*

3. Economic Realities

Women, on average, face:

- Lower lifetime earnings due to wage gaps and career breaks (e.g. caregiving).
- Greater likelihood of living longer (so their money must last further).
- Higher healthcare costs in old age.

These realities drive a greater focus on:

- Budgeting and savings discipline
- Emergency funds and insurance
- Low-risk, long-term financial planning

4. Risk Perception & Decision-Making Style

- Research shows women tend to analyse risks more carefully.
- They may ask more questions, seek advice, and avoid overconfidence.
- This results in:
    - Fewer investment mistakes
    - Lower portfolio volatility
    - Better long-term returns (on average)

It's not fear—it's measured caution.

5. Caretaking Roles

- Women are more often responsible for children, aging parents, and even spouses.
- This leads to prioritizing predictability, protection, and budget control—not just for themselves, but for those who depend on them.
- A mindset emerges: *"I can't afford to take chances with what others rely on."*

6. Trust and Confidence Gaps (Often Socially Imposed)

- Many women are not encouraged to feel confident with investing or finance.

- Financial services have historically been male-oriented, making some women feel unwelcome or under-informed.
- As a result, women often focus on what they can control: budgets, expenses, savings, and planning.

Here's a short table comparing how men and women may differ in financial thinking when it comes to Risk vs Stability:

Aspect	Men	Women
Risk Tolerance	Higher - willing to take big risks	Lower - prefer calculated, safe risks
Focus	Growth, returns, legacy	Security, consistency, planning
Investment Style	Aggressive, frequent trading	Conservative, long-term investing
Budgeting	Less emphasis on details	Strong focus on tracking & control
Financial Goal	Wealth building, status	Stability, protection, independence

Section 8: Fear of Losing Respect vs Fear of Losing Love

This is a deep and insightful contrast. The fear of losing respect versus the fear of losing love often reflects different emotional drivers and value systems in people—shaped by personality, upbringing, culture, and gender dynamics.

A Men fear disrespect more than anything.

Many men do fear disrespect more than almost anything else, and this insight helps explain a lot of behaviour in relationships, work, and personal identity.

Why Many Men Fear Disrespect

1. Identity Is Often Tied to Competence

- Boys are often taught: *"Be strong, be capable, be in control."*
- Respect becomes a symbol of worth, strength, and manhood.
- Disrespect = being seen as weak, irrelevant, or failing.

2. Masculinity Is Often Performance-Based

- Unlike love (which may be seen as unconditional), respect is earned.
- Many men grow up believing they must prove themselves–through success, dominance, or resilience.
- Fear: "If I lose respect, I lose everything I've worked to be."

3. Disrespect Feels Like Public Shame

- For men, disrespect isn't just a feeling–it's often social exposure.
- It threatens status and reputation, two things many men are conditioned to protect at all costs.

4. Cultural & Evolutionary Roots

- Across history, men's survival often depended on hierarchy and dominance–being respected meant safety, power, and opportunity.
- Disrespect could mean being challenged, replaced, or excluded.

B Women fear emotional disconnection or abandonment.

- Many women do deeply fear emotional disconnection or abandonment, and this fear often influences how they communicate, bond, and respond to stress in relationship

1. Attachment & Bonding: Biological and Emotional Roots

- From infancy, emotional connection = safety.
- Women are biologically wired for relational bonding (oxytocin release during touch, communication, and caregiving).
- Emotional closeness signals security, belonging, and stability.

So when that bond feels broken (through silence, neglect, or emotional distance), the brain may interpret it as:

"I'm not safe. I could be left."

2. Social Conditioning

- Girls are often taught to nurture, relate, and seek harmony.
- Many women grow up believing their value lies in being loved, liked, or chosen.

- As a result, emotional connection becomes central to identity.

The fear becomes: "If someone pulls away emotionally, I must not be enough."

3. Relational Sensitivity

- Studies show women often have a more active mirror neuron system (empathy processing), making them more attuned to changes in others' moods or behaviours.
- This means even small shifts in emotional tone (coldness, lack of eye contact, silence) can feel like emotional rejection.

4. Emotional Abandonment ≠ Physical Absence

- A person can be *physically present* but *emotionally absent*, and this triggers the same abandonment fear.
- Withdrawal, avoidance, or indifference can feel as painful as actual leaving.

5. Fear Often Rooted in Early Experiences

- Abandonment fears often stem from:
    - Emotionally unavailable parents
    - Unpredictable affection
    - Inconsistent love or validation
- These early patterns may create anxious attachment styles where the person fears:
    - Being too much

- Being left
- Not being loved enough

Comparison table for Fear of Losing Respect vs Fear of Losing Love:

Aspect	Fear of Losing Respect	Fear of Losing Love
Core Need	Status, strength, competence	Connection, acceptance, belonging
Common Emotion	Shame, inadequacy	Abandonment, loneliness
Typical Response	Defensiveness, control, withdrawal	People-pleasing, anxiety, overliving
Triggered By	Criticism, being ignored, failure	Rejection, coldness, emotional distance
Often Seen In	Men, leaders, high-achievers	Women, caregivers, emotionally sensitive people

Section 9: Dreams and Ambition: Whose Career Wins in a Relationship?

Dreams and Ambition: Whose Career Wins in a Relationship touches on one of the most emotionally charged and practical decisions couples face

A How society shapes men to prioritize career.

1 Provider Role Expectation: Men are traditionally expected to be the primary breadwinners, responsible for financially supporting their families. This cultural norm creates strong

pressure for men to focus on building successful careers to fulfil this role.

2 Masculinity Linked to Achievement: Society often equates manhood with achievement and status. For many men, professional success becomes a key part of their identity and self-esteem, motivating them to prioritize career advancement.

3 Cultural Reinforcement from Childhood: From a young age, boys are encouraged to be competitive, ambitious, and goal-oriented. This early socialization encourages a drive for achievement that naturally extends into their careers.

4 Media and Role Models: Movies, sports figures, and other media frequently celebrate men who demonstrate ambition and professional success. These role models reinforce the ideal that career achievement defines a man's value and leadership.

5 Peer and Family Pressure: Families and male peer groups often reinforce career ambition as a sign of maturity and respect. This social environment encourages men to measure themselves by their professional accomplishments

B How women face the conflict between career and caregiving.

1 Double Burden of Work and Home: Women frequently juggle full-time careers alongside the majority of caregiving responsibilities at home—childcare, eldercare, and household tasks—leading to physical and emotional exhaustion.

2 Career Sacrifices and Slowdowns: Many women pause, reduce hours, or step back from career advancement to meet

caregiving demands, which can impact long-term earnings, promotions, and professional growth.

3 Societal Expectations and Pressure: Social norms often expect women to be primary caregivers, creating guilt or judgment when they prioritize career ambitions or seek support in caregiving roles.

4 Workplace Challenges and Lack of Flexibility: Women face challenges such as, lack of flexible work options, and insufficient support for balancing caregiving, making it hard to maintain career momentum.

5 Emotional and Identity Conflict: Women often struggle internally with balancing their professional identity and personal caregiving role, feeling torn between aspirations and responsibilities, which can lead to stress and self-doubt

Section 10: Avoid Arguments

An argument is a disagreement or exchange of opposing views, often involving strong emotions like anger, frustration, or defensiveness. It usually happens when two or more people fail to understand, accept, or compromise with each other's opinions, beliefs, or expectations.

A How to Avoid Arguments with Women

In every relationship, communication is the bridge between understanding and misunderstanding. Men and women often approach emotions and expression differently. While men may prioritize logic and quick resolution, women often seek emotional validation and connection.

This difference can create friction–not because one side is wrong, but because they're speaking in different emotional languages.

Men may unknowingly trigger arguments by reacting too quickly, dismissing feelings, or trying to "fix" problems instead of simply listening. Women, in turn, may feel unheard, misunderstood, or emotionally disconnected–leading to frustration or conflict.

Avoiding arguments doesn't mean avoiding the truth.

It means learning how to respond instead of react, how to respect emotional space, and how to build trust even in moments of disagreement. When men adopt a more empathetic and emotionally intelligent approach, communication improves and relationships deepen.

The following strategies are not about manipulation. They are about mutual respect, patience, and the understanding that peace is more powerful than ego.

1. Listen Before You Speak

Women often feel frustrated not because of what's said, but because they feel unheard. Men tend to jump to solutions or defend themselves quickly.

Tip: Practice active listening–keep eye contact, nod, and wait until she finishes speaking before responding. Even a simple "I hear you" builds trust.

2. Acknowledge Emotions, Not Just Words

A woman's emotions are deeply tied to her communication. Ignoring her feelings can escalate any issue.

Tip: Say things like, “I can see that you're really hurt,” or “This seems important to you.”

This shows respect for her emotions, even if you don't fully agree with her logic.

3. Don’t React Instantly

Quick reactions, especially emotional ones, often cause more damage than the argument itself.

Tip: Pause, breathe, and take a moment to reflect before speaking.

You don’t need to respond in 2 seconds–sometimes silence is more powerful.

4. Find Common Ground

Winning an argument often means losing emotional connection. Women appreciate compromise more than confrontation.

Tip: Even if you disagree, find a part of her view you can agree with.

Example: “I agree I could’ve handled that differently.”

5. Never Say “Clampdown”

This phrase almost always backfires. It makes women feel dismissed or belittled.

Tip: Instead, say, “Let’s take a short break and talk when we’re both calmer” or, “I care about this–let’s not say things we’ll regret.”

Respect is more calming than commands.

6. Recognize the Real Issue

Sometimes the fight isn't about the topic at hand. It might be about past neglect, feeling unimportant, or emotional stress.

Tip: Ask deeper questions: "Is there something else bothering you?"

Often, understanding the root cause helps avoid repeated arguments.

7. Use Humour Carefully

Humour can lighten a situation–but it must be respectful.

Sarcasm, teasing, or mocking during a serious moment can feel insulting.

Tip: Gentle humour or light jokes can shift energy, but never use humour to avoid responsibility or dismiss her feelings.

8. Don't Aim to Win–Aim to Understand

Arguments aren't competitions. Trying to "win" can make a woman feel like you're fighting against her instead of with her.

Tip: Change your mindset. Ask: "What can I learn from this?"

Empathy is more valuable than ego in any relationship.

9. Appreciate, Even During Disagreement

Expressing appreciation softens emotional walls.

Tip: Even in tense moments, say: "I respect your honesty," or "I know you care, and I value that."

It reminds both of you that you're on the same team.

10. Set Calm Boundaries

If a conversation gets too intense, stepping back is not weakness–it's wisdom.

Tip: Calmly say, "I don't want to argue. Let's talk about this later when we're both calm

" This prevents emotional escalation and preserves respect.

Final Thought:

Avoiding arguments isn't about silence or submission–it's about smart emotional communication. When men learn to navigate emotional space with respect and patience, they earn not just peace–but deeper connection.

B How to Avoid Arguments with Men

While women may seek emotional expression and deeper conversation during conflict, men often process arguments differently. Many men value logic, clarity, and directness. They tend to shut down or withdraw when overwhelmed or emotionally cornered.

Understanding this difference is the key to avoiding unnecessary friction. Women can avoid arguments with men–not by suppressing their voice, but by delivering it in a way that connects, not confronts.

1. Speak Calmly, Not Emotionally

Men often tune out when conversations get emotionally intense. It's not that they don't care–they're just wired to process facts before feelings.

Tip: Use a calm, steady tone. Express your emotions with clarity, not with raised volume.

2. Be Direct and Clear

Men appreciate directness. Hints, passive remarks, or vague comments can confuse or frustrate them.

Tip: Say exactly what you feel or need.

Example: Instead of saying "You never help me," say "I'd really appreciate your help with dinner tonight."

3. Avoid Blame and Accusation

Phrases like "You always..." or "You never..." trigger defensiveness.

Tip: Use "I" statements.

Example: "I felt ignored when you didn't respond." This invite understanding, not resistance.

4. Give Him Time to Process

Men may not respond immediately–they need space to think and then talk.

Tip: Don't force him to speak in the heat of the moment. Say:

"Take your time. I'm here when you're ready to talk."

5. Don't Interrupt or Talk Over Him

Interrupting a man when he's finally expressing himself can shut him down completely.

Tip: Even if you disagree, let him finish. Then calmly share your view.

6. Show Respect, Even in Disagreement

Respect is one of the most valued things for a man. When he feels disrespected, he's more likely to argue.

Tip: Avoid sarcasm, criticism, or belittling language. Disagree with ideas, not character.

7. Pick the Right Time to Talk

Trying to talk when he's stressed, tired, or distracted will only lead to friction.

Tip: Wait for a calmer moment. Say:

"Can we talk about something important when you're not busy?"

8. Focus on Solutions, Not Drama

Men prefer solving problems over dwelling on emotions for too long.

Tip: After expressing how you feel, ask: "How do you think we can fix this?" It gives him something to do, which men often respond better to.

9. Acknowledge His Efforts

Sometimes, men feel unappreciated, even when they try. This hidden frustration can cause arguments.

Tip: Say things like: "I noticed you tried today, and I appreciate that." A little validation goes a long way.

10. Know When to Walk Away

If a man becomes too aggressive, loud, or disrespectful, staying and arguing can make it worse.

Tip: Exit with strength and calmness:

"Let's not talk like this. I'm walking away until we can both speak respectfully."

Final Thought:

Avoiding arguments with men is about strategic communication. Women don't need to become quiet—they need to become clear, calm, and confident. When men feel respected, they're more willing to listen, reflect, and respond with maturity.

The Silent Dinner

A story of misunderstanding, emotional need, and mental exhaustion between a woman and a man.

The Excitement

It was Friday morning. Meera woke up early, humming to herself. She had taken a half-day leave from work just to prepare a surprise dinner for Rohan. It had been a stressful few week—meetings, family issues, bills. She thought, "Maybe a quiet evening will bring us closer again."

She cleaned the house, bought fresh flowers, cooked his favourite meal, and even wore the blue saree he once said made her look "like peace itself."

But Rohan had no idea.

The Arrival

Rohan entered the house at 8:20 PM—later than usual. He looked tired. His shirt was crumpled, his face dull. The first thing he said was: "Traffic was a nightmare. And my boss just dumped three more tasks on me." He didn't notice the candles, the food, the flowers. His phone rang again. Without greeting Meera, he answered and walked to the balcony. "Yeah, I'm home. Let's get the numbers reviewed tonight.

"Meera stood frozen near the table, heart sinking.

The Quiet Storm

Meera waited. Ten minutes... then fifteen.

She moved the chapatis back to the hotplate to keep them warm. Still, no sign of Rohan. He was still on the call, pacing, now sounding annoyed. "It's not that simple, Rajeev. I can't just rewrite the entire report tonight. Meera's joy turned into frustration. "He can't even look at me? Am I that invisible?"

The Explosion

Rohan finally entered, put his phone down, and went straight to the sofa. Meera (sharp tone): "Dinner's been ready for 30 minutes. "Rohan (blunt): "Then why didn't you eat?" Meera: "I was waiting for you. I planned this evening... can't you see that?"

Rohan: "I didn't ask for a dinner plan. I had a hellish day, Meera."

Meera: "So I should suffer because you had a bad day? That's your excuse for ignoring me?"

The Thinking Gap

Rohan (raising voice): "I'm not ignoring you. I just needed a few minutes to breathe!"

Meera: "You always need space. But when do I get attention? When do I matter?"

Narration (Author's Insight):

This is where many arguments begin.

Meera wants emotional connection. Rohan wants mental recovery.

Both are valid—but they don't recognize each other's needs.

The Silence

They stopped talking. Rohan stared at the ceiling, angry. Meera sat on the chair; arms crossed. Two people. One room. A storm between them.

Meera's eyes welled up. Not because of the fight—but because she felt lonely, even in love. Rohan clenched his jaw, feeling misunderstood. "Why does she always see the worst in me? "Both were hurt. Neither knew how to break the silence.

The Reflection

Meera looked at the cold food. Her heart said, talk softly, but her ego said, let him suffer. Rohan glanced at her from the sofa. His mind said, she overreacted again, but his conscience whispered, you didn't even say thank you. Sometimes, we fight not because we hate—but because we care, and don't know how to show

The First Step

Rohan stood up and walked to the table. He picked up a plate.

Rohan: "I should've seen what you did. It's... beautiful. I'm sorry, Meera."

Meera didn't speak. She just looked up, surprised.

Rohan (gently): "Work drained me, but that's no excuse for ignoring your love."

Meera (softly): "I should've asked how your day was, before attacking you."

They sat down, side by side. Not enemies anymore.

The Connection

They began eating.

No music. No phones. Just food, eye contact,

and the sound of forgiveness.

Rohan: "You're right. I've been distant lately."

Meera: "And I've been craving attention, maybe a bit too much."

They both smiled, shyly. Sometimes maturity is not about avoiding conflict, but knowing how to end it with love.

The Lesson

Narration (Author's Voice):

Arguments between men and women are not battles—they are clashes of emotional timing.

She needed him to notice. He needed her to understand.

In that simple dinner, they didn't just share a meal—they shared their differences. And in that, they found connection.

Because in the war of minds, peace is not silence—it is understanding.

Einstein's Silent Brain

When Albert Einstein breathed his last in 1955, the world wept for the man who had bent time and space with his mind. Newspapers wrote about his discoveries, about relativity and the universe, but very few knew of the strange journey that began the moment his body left this world.

In a quiet hospital room, Dr. Thomas Harvey opened Einstein's skull. He did something unusual, even shocking—he removed the brain of the greatest thinker of the century. At first, this was a secret. Later, with hesitant approval from Einstein's family, the brain was cut into pieces and studied by scientists for decades.

But here is where the story surprises us: the brain of the genius was not giant, not glowing, not different in some magical way. It weighed as much as an ordinary brain. And yet, in its hidden folds, there were small peculiarities—slightly broader connections between the two halves, unusual patterns in the parietal lobes. These differences sparked endless debates. Did these folds make Einstein a genius? Or did his genius make us look at those folds differently?

The Puzzle of Brilliance

Science often looks for physical evidence of greatness. We want to believe that genius must leave a fingerprint inside the brain's tissue. But Einstein himself rejected such narrow thinking. He once said: "I have no special talent. I am only passionately curious."

What if the true secret of his brilliance was not in the size of his brain, but in the way he used it? Not in anatomy, but in attitude. His brain was a battlefield where imagination danced with logic, where equations were painted like art, and where the laws of physics were felt like poetry.

Einstein and the War of Minds

This mystery speaks directly to the "mind war" between men and women. Society often tags men as logical and women as emotional, men as analytical and women as intuitive. But Einstein's mind refused to stay on one side. He thought like a scientist, but dreamed like a poet. He solved problems with logic, but also trusted imagination.

Perhaps the unusual bridges inside his brain allowed him to do what we all struggle with—combine the male and female styles of thinking into one powerful harmony.

The Real Lesson

So, what do we learn from Einstein's silent brain? That genius is not about possession of a unique organ, but about balance. A balance of order and chaos, numbers and dreams, logic and feeling.

His preserved brain may rest in glass jars, but the real Einstein lives on as a reminder: each of us holds a mind capable of brilliance if we dare to connect the pieces within us. The true "war of minds" is not between genders but inside every human being—a war between the left and right, between logic and intuition. Victory comes not in choosing one, but in uniting both.

The Whisper of Einstein's Brain

(A fictional dialogue to bring the mystery alive)

The room was silent. In a glass jar rested the preserved fragments of Einstein's brain–silent, yet echoing with the memory of thought. Suddenly, as if imagination itself gave it a voice, the brain spoke.

Reader: "Tell me, what was your secret? Why did you see the universe differently than the rest of us?"

Einstein's Brain: "Secret? There was none. My folds and ridges look ordinary to scientists. But genius is not carved in flesh–it is born in curiosity. I was never afraid to ask 'Why?' even when no one else cared to ask."

Reader: "But they say your brain had unusual connections between its two halves. Did that make you different?"

Einstein's Brain: "Perhaps. But what use are bridges if one never crosses them? I walked between logic and imagination, between numbers and dreams. Most people live only on one shore of the mind. I built my life on both."

Reader: "And what about men and women? Do they think differently because their brains are shaped differently?"

Einstein's Brain: "Differences, yes. Limitations, no. A woman may listen to her heart; a man may follow reason. But the greatest strength lies in blending both. My ideas were not born from logic alone. They were born when reason danced with imagination, when science held hands with wonder."

Reader: "So, what lesson do you leave for us?"

Einstein's Brain (whispering):

"Do not worship me. Do not worship the jar I rest in. Instead, look within your own mind. Your brain too has bridges—between left and right, between thought and feeling. Dare to cross them. That is where genius hides."

"Two Halves of the Same Sky"

He stands like stone, yet carries storms,
Weathered by years, reshaped by norms.
His silence speaks, though words are few,
A heart of fire, a soul most true.

She walks with grace, yet roars like flame,
Unbent by sorrow, unbound by name.
Her tears are strength, her smile a sword,
In quiet battles, she's never ignored.

They rise, they fall, they break, they mend–
Not rivals, no–just different ends
Of one great thread that weaves the light,
Both day and dusk, both wrong and right.

He may not cry where all can see,
But feels as deep as any sea.
She may not shout to make her stand,
But builds the world with steady hand.

Together not to lead or follow–
But side by side, both fierce and hollow.
Each one whole, yet more complete
When heart meets heart, and strength meets sweet.

So let no voice divide their worth,
They're born of stars, they share this earth.
Man and woman–fire and rain,
Two halves of love, both joy and pain.

TWO MINDS, ONE WORLD

Men and women think differently – yet they live, love, and dream in the same world.

This book uncovers the hidden battles and unspoken truths of how their minds work.

It is not about who is right or wrong – it is about understanding the contrasts, embracing the differences, and finding harmony in the war of thoughts.

If you've ever wondered why he acts so logically, why she feels so deeply, or why the gap between them sometimes feels impossible to cross – this book will give you the answers.

Mind War is not just a study of men and women. It is a journey to acceptance, empathy, and love.

A Message from the Author

Some wars are fought with words. Some with silence. And some... inside glass buildings where smiles decide your future.

Mind War: How Men and Women Think Differently was born from observing emotions, psychology, and the invisible battles between hearts and minds. It speaks about how men and women think, react, love, clash, and coexist. But there is another battlefield I could not ignore.

The corporate world.

Behind polished presentations and motivational slogans lies a reality few talk about openly where truth is often inconvenient, loyalty is measured by usefulness, and ethics quietly wait outside closed meeting rooms.

This upcoming book, Corporate Politics, is not written to impress. It is written to expose. It speaks for those who were silenced. It questions systems that reward noise over integrity. It challenges cultures where survival matters more than character If Mind War helps you understand people,

Corporate Politics will help you understand power.

This book is for: The honest professional who was overlooked The silent performer who was replaced by a louder face The dreamer who entered corporate life with values—and paid a price for it This is not a guide on how to play politics. This is a mirror showing why politics exists.

I believe books should not just entertain—they should shake something inside you. If this page made you pause, question, or feel uncomfortable, then the conversation has already begun.

Corporate Politics (The Unspoken Truth of Corporate Life) Coming soon